THIRD EDITION

ESSAYS

that will get you into

Law School

Adrienne Dowhan, Chris Dowhan, and Dan Kaufman

BARRON'S

All inquiries should be addressed to:
Barron's Educational Series, Inc.
250 Wireless Boulevard
Hauppauge, NY 11788
www.barronseduc.com

Library of Congress Catalog Card No. 2009010384

ISBN-13: 978-0-7641-4229-1
ISBN-10: 0-7641-4229-1

Library of Congress Cataloging-in-Publication Data
Dowhan, Adrienne.
    Essays that will get you into law school / by Adrienne Dowhan, Chris Dowhan, Daniel Kaufman.—3rd ed.
        p.   cm.
    Includes index.
    ISBN-13: 978-0-7641-4229-1
    ISBN-10: 0-7641-4229-1
    1. Law schools—United States—Entrance examinations—Study guides.
I. Dowhan, Chris. II. Kaufman, Daniel, 1968–   III. Title.
KF285.Z9K38 2009
340.071'173—dc22
                                                                2009010384

Printed in the United States of America
9 8 7 6 5 4 3 2 1

Contents

Acknowledgments

The authors of this book are all part of an Internet-based company called IvyEssays. Since its creation in 1996, IvyEssays' goal has been to help students gain admission to leading colleges and graduate schools by providing them with a variety of resources such as examples of previously successful essays and professional editing services.

We owe our sincere thanks to two groups of people. First there are all the students who have permitted us to publish their admissions essays so they might light the way for future rounds of hopeful applicants. Second, there is the team of IvyEssays contributors—past and present admissions officers and professional writers who together have logged more than 50 years of admissions experience. This series would not have been possible without the assistance of those cited below:

Miriam Ruth Albert is Assistant Professor of Legal and Ethical Studies at Fordham University Schools of Business. She was Legal Methods Professor and Associate Director of Admissions at Widener University School of Law where she counseled prospective applicants and evaluated more than 400 applications. She also taught an LSAT preparation course for Stanley Kaplan Educational Center.

Amy Engle worked at the Hofstra University School of Law for more than seven years and served there as Assistant Dean of Admissions.

Helen LaFave is an independent consultant who counsels prospective students through all stages of the admissions process. She has also served as Senior Programs Officer and Recruitment Program Officer at Columbia University where she helped numerous students through extensive graduate school application processes.

Amy Yerkes was an instructor at the University of Maryland School of Medicine where she taught a course designed to increase the writing skills of prospective medical students for the Office of Minority Student Affairs. She has taught at the University of Pennsylvania and is currently Assistant to the Dean at Johns Hopkins University School of Continuing Studies and a lecturer at Western Maryland College.

Joanna Henderson has been Director of Graduate Admissions responsible for MBA programs at Babson, Dean of Admissions at Colby-Sawyer College, and, most recently, Director of the New England Admissions Office at Marietta College in Ohio. She is also an advisor/consultant for Kaplan.

Thomas Vance Sturgeon has more than eight years' experience in admissions as Associate Director of Admissions at Duke University and Assistant Director of Admissions at Guilford College. He is currently Director of Admissions and College Placement at the South Carolina School for Science and Mathematics. Mr. Sturgeon is a widely published author and lecturer on the subject of college admissions, and has been quoted in *Money Magazine's Guide to Colleges* and published in the *Journal of College Admissions.*

Marcy Whaley is the former Associate Director of Admissions at the College Institute of Technology and Assistant Dean of Admissions at Illinois Institute of Technology. She has more than a decade of experience in college admissions and is presently an independent admissions consultant and freelance technical writer.

Scott Anderson is Associate Director of Admissions at Cornell University. His past experience includes the position of Assistant Director of Admissions at Vassar College, and he has been on the admissions staffs at the University of Vermont, St. Michael's College, and the University of Virginia.

Patricia M. Soares is an independent educational consultant for underprivileged youth and has many years of experience as an admissions officer. She has been Assistant Director of Admissions at Connecticut College and an admissions officer at Rhode Island College.

IvyEssays was founded based on the belief that some people have more access than others to the resources and information that improve one's chances of getting into the top schools. While admissions officers do their best to take these disparities into account, it is up to students to equip themselves for the application process to the best of their abilities. IvyEssays hopes that its services can help level the admissions playing field by providing resources that might otherwise be available only to the privileged. Good luck and good writing!

Introduction

Your Personal Statement—Why All the Fuss?

How would you feel if getting into the law school of your choice had nothing to do with your grades and your test scores? Imagine for a moment that the only thing an admissions committee is ever going to see is your essay. Two pages, double-spaced are all they will have to make a decision that will change the rest of your life.

Does this make you elated or nervous? Or a little of both? In any case, consider this during the writing process: Everything you have done up to now is completed—past tense. You couldn't change it if you wanted to, so don't worry about it. But even if you have strong test scores and a good undergraduate record, this is not the time to rest on your laurels. The personal statement—the essay—lies ahead; treat it as if it is the only thing that matters. As one admissions officer stated:

The essay is the only aspect of the application over which the applicant still has total control.

The personal statement brings your application to life. Think of it as the face of your application. Without it, you are little more than a statistic, just another faceless person in a crowd.

The admissions committee wants, above all, to see a real person. Because law schools don't interview, the essay is virtually the only tool you have to bring your application to life, making you human, memorable, and "accept"able.

An application with a poorly written essay doesn't give admissions officers the opportunity to care. It's basic psychology: Make them feel that they know you, and it will be harder for them to reject you. Make them know you and like you, and they might accept you despite weaknesses in other areas.

The essay gives the applicants a chance to showcase their strengths beyond simply the numbers. In other words: sure, they have a high GRE and impressive LSAT scores but at some point we're going to ask: "What else?"

Showcasing your strengths means more than just flaunting a list of qualifications and experience. An essay can demonstrate motivation, maturity, depth of character, the ability to think clearly and logically, a sense of humor, leadership ability, confidence, intelligence, and professionalism. Whatever your strengths are, here is the one place where you can shout them out. And if you succeed in writing an essay that demonstrates all of the above, you have probably also written your ticket into the school of your choice.

Understanding the importance of the essay is a necessary first step toward writing an effective one, but that knowledge alone won't do you a whole lot of good. In fact, it could even hurt your chances if all it does is make you nervous. So, if all of this has you perspiring, you can relax now. Taking the essay seriously is the first step. We're here to help you get through the rest of them.

What We've Done

We have developed a powerful program to help you write an effective essay. We will give you the tools that you need coupled with a strategy that works. We will help you define the goals of your essay, get the words on paper, and polish it to perfection. Here is a sample of what lies ahead:

1. **Preparation and Strategy:** Before you can begin writing, you need to devise a plan of attack. You need to understand your audience (who are the admissions officers and what do they want?) and you need to understand yourself (honestly assess your strengths, motivations, and goals). Then we'll show you how to use the information you've gathered to strategize on a theme that complements the rest of your application.

2. **Writing:** Once you've done some research, defined your goals, and chosen a topic, it is time for you to begin writing. We will get you through even the worst case of writer's block and help you develop a structure for presenting your ideas in a solid first draft.

3. **Making It Perfect:** This last step is crucial. We will show you how to take that first draft and work it to perfection. You'll need to write and rewrite, think and write again, until your essay is worthy of being the face of your application.

Armed with this step-by-step program, you will have everything you need to make the best possible impression on the admissions committee. Remember that right now your personal statement is the most important part of your application because it is still within your control. With that in mind, let's get started.

A Note About Plagiarism

Throughout this book, we have emphasized the need for honest, personal application essays. To submit anything else to the schools you are applying to is not only stupid—it's illegal.

If you do borrow material from other sources, be sure to credit it properly. If you are not careful about this, you may hurt your chances at getting into a particular school. To purposely avoid giving credit where credit is due is to court disaster.

In Chapter 1, an admissions officer is quoted as saying, "After fifteen years of reading hundreds of essays a year, you develop an amazing ability to see straight through the bull." This is also true of detecting plagiarism. Admissions officers *do* read hundreds of essays every year. In doing so, they have developed a sense of whether or not the author of the essay is being honest. Although it may sound impossible, these admissions officers also tend to remember many of the essays that they read. If it is discovered that you have "borrowed" someone else's essay, you will undoubtedly be denied admission.

You owe it to yourself to be honest, forthright, and sincere.

PART ONE

Preparation and Strategy

Chapter Highlights

- You are writing specifically to admissions officers – know what they want.

- Personal statements must express your motivation for attending law school.

- The most effective personal statements are actually *personal*.

- Good writing skills must be showcased.

Do's and Don'ts

- Do tell stories.

- Don't use gimmicks.

- Do be completely honest.

- Don't be boring.

- Do use details.

- Do get feedback.

CHAPTER 1

Assess Your Audience

Every time you give out information—whether consciously or not, you must assess your audience—and modify your delivery based on that audience. Are you writing for strangers, acquaintances, or friends? If they are strangers, what will they know about you beforehand? What are their interests and biases? What are their expectations? If these questions aren't answered before you begin preparation, you will have considerable difficulty deciding what to say, let alone the manner in which to say it. After all, you would not address a Girl Scout troop in the same way as a member of the U.S. Supreme Court. Now apply the same commonsense approach to your personal statement.

In this chapter we pose the questions that you should be asking about your audience, to your audience. In other words, we went out into the field and asked a variety of admissions officers at some of the top law schools in the United States for the answers to such questions as:

1. Who are you?

2. What do you look for in an essay?

3. What are you tired of finding?

By the end of this chapter you should be familiar with the major do's and don'ts of writing an essay as defined by the very people who will later be reading and judging your essay. Think of these tips as guideposts to help you navigate through a vast array of options on theme, strategy, and presentation.

Who Is Your Audience? A Profile of the Admissions Committee

Every law school has a core of individuals who make up the admissions committee. This committee is generally a mix of admissions staff, faculty members, and lawyers. While the structure and makeup of the committee is going to be different at every law school, your application will follow a similar path at all of them. First, it will be read in its entirety by one of the members of the committee. Depending on the school, this could be the Dean of Admissions, a junior member of the admissions staff, or a faculty member (any of whom could be and usually are lawyers themselves). Either way, you can be sure that your entire application will be read thoroughly by at least one, and more likely by two or three different people. The means that, despite rumors to the contrary, your application will never be dismissed based on any one single factor such as GPA or LSAT scores.

We asked admissions officers how much time they usually spend looking at each essay the first time through, and the answers ranged from 3 to 15 minutes.

If the essay is either very good or very bad, a handful of minutes can be all it takes. Then again, on a busy day a handful of minutes can be all we have to give.

We asked them how many statements they read in a day and their answers were even more surprising: Admissions officers can (and often do) plow through 40 to 50 essays a day during peak weeks. This means that the same two pages that may take you days or even weeks to put together are going to get only a few minutes of attention and are going to have to stand out in a crowd of dozens of others read in the same day.

So, much as we hate to say it, your personal statement really needs to function both as an essay and as an advertisement. If you're not convinced, then ask yourself this: When was the last time you read over a dozen short stories in a day, spending only a few minutes on each one? Now ask: When was the last time you spent a few minutes each on a dozen or more commercials in a day? While this does not mean that your statement should be gimmicky, or cutesy, or include a sing-a-long song, it does mean that the best essays, like the best ads, are going to be interesting enough to grab the readers' attention on the first read and powerful enough to hold it even if it is the fortieth essay they have read that day. However, unlike an ad, a good essay will also withstand longer, more in-depth scrutiny.

Yes and No Piles

Once an application has been given a first read, it will go into one of roughly three piles. The Yes and the No piles will be made up mainly of people whose numbers (GPA and LSAT scores) are extreme in either direction, and whose essay and experience back up the impression the numbers have made.

The vast majority of applicants fall into the third pile. The longer your application lasts in this pile the more alike (in terms of numbers) it will begin to look to all the others that are there. After a point it becomes impossible for the committee to make numbers-based decisions, and they hone in on the "softer" sides of the application. This is the pile that gets the most attention and passes through the most hands, so the longer your application is retained, the more scrutiny your essay will get. It is for this that you write—because after a certain point your essay becomes virtually the only tool you have to distinguish yourself from the rest of the homogenous crowd.

What Is the Committee Looking For?

When members of an admissions committee look at your file as a whole (transcripts, LSAT scores, application, recommendations, and personal statement), what they seek is essentially the same. Can this person succeed academically at this school and will this person make a good attorney upon graduating?

But when the committee members hone in on your essay, the focus shifts from the quantifiable and objective to the nebulous and subjective. The admissions officers we spoke with, for example, said that they looked to the essays to feel that they have gotten to know the personality and character of a real, live human being. As one officer put it: "I'm going to spend the next three years with this person. I'm going to choose someone I feel I know, and someone I feel I could like."

Motivation

The admissions committee will expect your essay to have answered the obvious, but not so simple, question "why?" They look to your essay to understand your motivation and assess your commitment to studying law.

Every essay should focus on answering the question, Why? In other words: Why law? Why now? Why here? Why us? And, of course, Why you?

You will be offered a lot of advice in the following pages, with plenty of do's and don'ts. In the midst of all of this, whatever you do, do not lose sight of the ultimate goal of the essay: You must convince the admissions committee members that you belong at their school. Everything we tell you should be used as a means to this end, so step back from the details of this process regularly and remind yourself of the big picture.

Writing/Communication Skills

Another obvious function of the essay is to showcase your *language abilities* and *writing skills*.

Your essay doesn't need to peg you as a future author or scholar, but as a future lawyer, judge, or politician. That said, the ability to communicate ideas and to present them skillfully is essential to success in the legal profession, and good writing stems from these good communication skills.

At this level, good writing skills are not sought, they are expected. So, while a beautifully written essay alone isn't going to get you into law school, a poorly written one could keep you out.

Does the candidate have a strong command of the English language, a solid writing style, and an ability to organize his or her thoughts? These are factors that are important to your success as a student, so why wouldn't they be important in an essay?

A Real Person

As we mentioned earlier, what our admissions panel said it seeks more than anything else in the personal statement is a real, live human being:

Please, show us your face! Don't do it for us—do it for yourselves. After all, a person is a lot easier to accept than a bunch of impersonal numbers and a list of accomplishments.

In light of this, then, it might not surprise you that when we asked admissions officers and law students for their number one piece of advice regarding the essay, we received the same response almost every time. Although it was expressed in many different ways (be honest, be sincere, be unique, be personal, and so on), it always came down to the same point: Be Yourself!

Admissions officers have to read tons of essays, and like anyone would, we get bored. The essays that interest us and that do the job right are the ones that show us who this person is.

Unfortunately, achieving this level of communication in writing does not come naturally to everyone. But that does not mean it cannot be learned. Four tips for achieving the kind of sincerity that the committees seek are listed below.

Remember, though, that even with the help of the tips and advice, the impression that your composition makes can be very hard to gauge in your own writing. It is a good idea to have objective people— preferably people who do not already know you well—read it over when you have finished. Ask them to describe the kind of person they pictured as they were reading. How accurate is their description relative to the one you were trying to present? If their description sounds ambiguous or if they are struggling for words, take it as a tip that you may not be presenting a clear and focused portrait.

Get Personal

The best way to write yourself into your statement is to make it personal. When you do this, your essay will automatically be more interesting and engaging, helping it stand out from the hundreds of others the committee will be reviewing that week.

Personalize your essay as much as possible; generic essays are not only boring to read, they're a waste of time because they don't tell you anything about the applicant that helps you get to know them better.

What does it mean to make your essay personal? It means that you drop the formalities and write about something that is truly meaningful to you. It means that you include a story or anecdote taken from your life, using ample detail and colorful imagery to give it life. And it means, above all, being completely honest.

Express thoughts and emotions, not just facts and ideas. Communicate real experiences. We want to know what has touched you in your life.

Part Two of this book contains many examples of essays that get personal. Look at Essay 38, for example. The writer begins by pointing out what an impersonal account of his life might look like, with his dean's list placement and near-perfect GPA, but the first line of his second paragraph carries through on his promise of "the whole story" with: "I was a short, thin fifth grader with a humiliating bionator jutting from my mouth." By giving us "the whole story" and discussing the deeply personal subject of his childhood insecurities, he makes his accomplishments far more meaningful, poignant, and memorable, and sets himself apart from all the other applicants with similarly stellar academic records. This is a perfect example of putting a face on an application. His first paragraph gives us the statistics, the awards, the accomplishments. The rest does exactly what an essay should do—it gives us a real human being.

Do keep in mind, however, that a story does not need to be poignant or emotional to be personal.

A personal epiphany, tragedy, life change, or earth-shattering event is not essential to a strong essay.

It is a small minority of students who have truly had a life-changing event to write about. In fact, students who rely too heavily on these weighty experiences often do themselves an injustice. They often don't think about what has really touched them or interests them because they are preoccupied with the topic that they think will impress the committee. They write overemotionally about death or another life drama because they think this will make them seem introspective and mature. What often happens, however, is that they rely on the experience itself to speak for them and never specifically explain how it changed them or give a solid example of how the emotional response makes meaningful their desire to attend law school. In other words, they don't make it personal.

Details, Details, Details

To make your essay personal, use details.

Generality is the death of good writing.

Focus on the little things, the details that make your story special and unique.

Using detail means getting *specific*. Show, don't tell, who you are by backing up each and every claim you make with real experiences. It is these details that make your story unique and interesting. Although it is true that the use of excessive detail can bog down the pace of a story, don't even think about limiting the amount that you incorporate during the first phases of writing. Too much detail in your writing is a much less likely pitfall than the alternative. To begin, err on the side of too much information and you can trim it down later. This way you won't find yourself manufacturing details to fit neatly into an essay you thought was complete, but that turned out to be less than engaging.

Look at the detail used by the writer of Essay 20, for example. He opens his essay with:

> *One evening, during Christmas vacation of my freshman year in college, when a formidable storm outside called for an evening of hot tea and heavy reading, I picked up a book that had been sitting on my desk for several weeks.*

Notice that he didn't just sit down and pick up a book. He sat down *during Christmas vacation,* and not just any year, but his *freshman year in college,* and it wasn't just any night, it was a stormy night that *called for an evening of hot tea and heavy reading* and the book wasn't just anywhere, it was on his desk and it had been there *for several weeks.* Notice too in the rest of his essay that he backs up each point he makes with specific examples. For example, he learned to value work and education from his father—a common claim—but he goes on to tell us exactly how his father taught him this by naming specific jobs and promotions he had. Details bring the experience to life.

Tell a Story

Incorporating a story into your essay can be a great way to make it interesting and enjoyable. The safest and most common method of integrating a story into an essay is to *tell the story* first, then step back into the role of narrator and explain why it was presented and what lessons were learned. The reason this method works is that it forces you to begin with the action, which is a sure way to get the readers' attention and keep them reading.

Many of the essay examples in this book make effective use of storytelling. They integrate the story into the essay to varying degrees. Essayist 28 takes one extreme by actually separating the narrative from the rest of her essay. She begins with two different stories told one after the other in one paragraph each, then skips a few lines on the paper and begins the "real" essay. Throughout his essay, Essayist 19 integrates his story of his efforts to ban the Confederate flag from the Boy Scouts, but steps out of the narrative at various points to discuss his more recent activities and his motivation to attend law school. The writer of Essay 7 takes the riskiest approach by doing nothing but tell her story of being cured of an illness in Kenya. She does not step out into the role of narrator even once, but leaves the reader to draw conclusions instead.

Be Honest!

This last point comes with no caveats, and should be upheld without exception. Nothing could be more simple, more straightforward, or more crucial than this: Be honest, forthright, and sincere. Admissions officers have zero tolerance for hype. If you try to be something that you're not, it will be transparent to the committee. You will give the impression of being immature at best and unethical at worst.

If you think you know what we want and you are trying to write to that, forget about it. There is nothing more obvious, and more humiliating, than doing a bad job of being someone else. Just be yourself and let us do the deciding.

When you are honest about your motivations and goals, you will come across as more personable and real. The writer of Essay 1, for example, strikes the reader as being completely straightforward and honest about everything he writes, from the effect that his childhood tics had on him to his initial distaste for Capitol Hill and law jargon. Because he was so honest in his assessments, his motivation for attending law school is never questioned and the impression of a sincere and upright individual is sealed.

What the Committees Are Tired of Finding

This should be obvious, but much of what admissions officers hate to find is simply the converse of the qualities they hope to get. In other words, don't try to be something you're not, don't bore them to tears, and don't hand in a poorly written, ill-constructed document riddled with typos and grammatical errors. There were, however, a few don'ts that came up so many times on our admissions officers' lists of pet peeves that they bear repeating. After all, they wouldn't be pet peeves if people weren't still doing them.

Don't Be Gimmicky

The first don't is the one that was named most often: Don't give in to gimmicks. The consensus among our admissions team was clear: "What might have been cute at the college level of admissions simply won't cut it at this level of competition." Although it is true that being creative is different from being cutesy, most of our staff agreed that even a creative approach that is pulled off well is risky:

When the creative approach works, it always seems like a great idea. But the tough part is that the admissions committee is made of many types of personalities, some formal and old school, and some more modern. The odds of a new, creative approach appealing to all (or even a majority) of these personalities is slim.

Here are a few attention-getters that definitely flopped:

I recall an essay that was made up of multi-pages, perhaps 20, print-outs of pie charts and graphs showing this candidate's maturity and skill levels in various scenarios, sometimes comparing him to his earlier self, and sometimes comparing him with his peers. It was a wacky idea, and it took far too long to figure out what the graphs and charts were supposed to indicate.

I remember an applicant who included an audiotape as her essay. It was a simulated interview on why she should get into law school. It came complete with a score and various sound effects simulating a courtroom. The problem? For one, I had to find a taperecorder and play it. But worse, the interview itself was fairly silly. The candidate didn't do herself much good with this particular creative approach.

Don't Be Dull!

Don't plan on toning it down too much, because the other extreme was considered to be just as bad. In other words: Don't Be Dull! Dullness was defined in numerous ways by our admissions advisors. All of them took issue with essays that did little more than recapitulate other parts of the application or provide lists of accomplishments. Your personal statement should not be an elongated résumé.

Listings of anything are dull, no matter how impressive they might look to you at the time. Save them for the other parts of your application.

There is a practical side to this, too: When you save your lists for your statement, you are wasting valuable space. It doesn't look good when you squander virtually the only opportunity you have to come across to the committee as a person.

Also labeled boring were essays that make excuses instead of giving honest and sincere explanations.

If the applicant wants to explain about a bad grade or low score, that's okay, but too often the excuses are lame and the candidate comes across as whiny.

Take note of this word, *whiny*. It came up with surprising regularity when officers were asked to describe the common pitfalls of applicant writing. If you have to explain a gap in your record, do it briefly and sincerely and move on quickly to the rest of your points.

Remember too that the length of your essay will be directly proportionate to the duration of the reader's yawn. Keep it short; not only will the admissions officers thank you, but your statement will likely become stronger and more focused during the culling process.

Mind the Mechanics

This should be so obvious that it doesn't need mentioning, but according to our admissions staff some applicants still aren't getting the message. There is simply no excuse for careless errors that could be easily caught by proofreading. One shocker that all our staff could relate to was the all-too-common mistake of forgetting to replace the proper name of the school throughout the statement. Every year Harvard gets essays beginning "The reason I want to attend Stanford Law . . ."

Here is more advice given by admissions staff:

Proofread! Have others proofread! Spell check! It's amazing how many people have careless, even really obvious typos in their statements. It makes the applicant look sloppy, uninterested, unintelligent.

Don't cram your essay onto the page with a tiny font. If I can't read it without a magnifying glass, I won't read it at all.

Stay away from lots of SAT-type big vocabulary words. It's obvious which applicants wrote their essays with the thesaurus in hand.

Get Feedback!

This has been mentioned several times already but it bears repeating: It is imperative that you get feedback about your essay before submitting your final version. For a variety of reasons, many of the don'ts listed above are hard to spot in your own writing. Find an honest, objective person to read the entire essay set for each school. As comforting as it might be, do not accept "they're great!" as feedback.

Do not rely on only one person's opinion, especially if you know the person well or disagree with the points that person has made. Even the most objective readers have their own set of biases and opinions, and no one person can accurately predict the reception your writing will have at the school to which you are applying.

One way to offset this potential risk is to make one of your evaluations a professional one. In addition to our web site (www.ivyessays.com), a number of qualified services can be found on the Internet.

Keep in mind that almost everyone gets feedback on their essays. Seeking that help from professionals assures that the advice you are getting on essay content is based on evidence of what admissions committees are looking for and that grammatical feedback is coming from people with solid editorial experience. The authors of this book, with help from admissions officers and experienced editors, created a website for this purpose. At *Ivyessays.com*, you can upload your essay and choose different levels of feedback depending on where you are in the writing process. If you are only in the rough draft phase of putting your thoughts to-gether, you can submit your essay for "quick feedback." You don't need to worry about the grammar or mechanics at this stage. Editors will focus on the content of your essay and will send you tips and advice on how to improve it. If you are further along in the process, you can submit the essay for a "full edit" and editors will help you polish your essay to perfection.

CHAPTER 2

Gather Your Material

Chapter Highlights

- Use brainstorming exercises to help devise essay topics.
- Assess yourself by writing down experiences, accomplishments, skills, and personality traits.
- Make notes of your major influences.
- Clearly identify your goals.
- Scan your notes for the topics that best describe you and your motivations.
- Identify the topics that would make the most interesting essay.

Now that you have a better understanding of your readers and some of their opinions on what makes an essay exceptional, you may feel ready to begin writing. You may even feel inspired about a particular topic or have some good ideas for how to present it. But before you begin, stop for a moment and assess your situation.

Creating an essay full of imagery and detail will require you to think carefully and thoroughly about your subject matter. This means much more than simply having a sense of the impression you want to make or an inspiration about a topic. It means, first and foremost, that you know yourself. Interesting, reflective, and revealing essays are always the result of careful self-analysis. It means, secondly, that you understand the specific points you will make in your essay, and thirdly, that you have identified concrete details to use in support of each.

We often forget the details of our lives over time, yet it is these details that provide the material for your essay, making it vibrant and alive. This chapter contains a number of brainstorming activities designed to help you get to know yourself better and gather the material you will need to write a colorful essay.

We begin with the basics in Start Your Engines. The exercises in this section will offer solutions to open the channels of your mind and get your pen moving. If you are not having a problem getting started, you might want to skip this section and go straight to Assess Yourself.

Start Your Engines

To get the most benefit out of this section, put your anxieties aside. Do not think about what the admissions committee wants, or worry about grammar or style or what anyone would think of your ideas. Worries like these hamper spontaneity and creativity. Focus instead on writing quickly and recording every thought you have the instant you have it. You will know that you are performing these exercises correctly if you are relaxing and having fun.

The Inventory

This exercise is designed to get your pen moving. The goal is simply to compile an inventory of your activities and accomplishments—school, sports, extracurricular activities, awards, work, and pastimes. You may have already made a similar list during the application process. If so, start with that list and try to add to it. This list will become fodder for topics to use when writing your personal statement. During this exercise you do not need to write down any qualities, skills, or feelings associated with the activities. For now it is more important to be completely comprehensive in the breadth of topics and items you include. For example, if you taught yourself chess or particularly enjoy occasional chess games with your uncle, you do not need to be in a chess club or have won a trophy to add it to the list. Think of how you spend your time each and every day, and include any items that seem significant to you. Spend no less than twenty minutes writing, and keep going for up to an hour if you can. If you run out of items quickly, don't worry—you will probably come up with more during the other exercises.

Stream of Consciousness

Take 20 minutes to answer each of the questions: Who are you? and What do you want? Start with whatever comes to mind first, and write without stopping for the entire time. Do not limit yourself to any one area of your life such as your career. Just let yourself go, be honest, and have fun. You might be surprised by what kind of results can come from this type of free association.

Morning Pages

If you have the discipline to practice this technique for a week, you may end up doing it for the rest of your life: Keep paper and a pen at your bedside. Set your alarm clock 20 minutes early, and when you are still in bed and groggy with sleep, start writing. Write about anything that comes to mind, as fast as you can, and do not stop until you have filled a page or two.

Journal Writing

Keep a journal for a few weeks, especially if you are stuck and your brainstorming seems to be going nowhere. Record not what you do each day, but your responses and thoughts to each day's experiences.

Top Tens

Write down your top ten favorites in the following areas: movies, books, plays, sports, paintings, historical eras, famous people. Step back and look at the lists objectively. What do they say about you? Do you see a pattern, or do any particular passions present themselves? And lastly, have any of your favorites had a significant effect on your outlook, opinions, or direction?

Free-Flow Writing

Choose one word that seems to appear on many of your questions such as *influence*, *strengths*, *career*, *diversity*, or *goals* and brainstorm around that word. Set a timer for 10 minutes and write, without stopping, everything you can think of that relates to the topic, including any single words that come to mind.

Assess Yourself

If the exercises in the last section have successfully stimulated your thoughts and animated your pen, then it is time to impose more focus on your brainstorming. These next exercises will help you do just that. They are more focused on finding the specific points and details that you will need to incorporate into your statement. But be sure to retain the open mind and creative attitude fostered in the last section.

The Chronological Method

Start from childhood and record any and all special or pivotal experiences that you remember. Go from grade to grade, and job to job, noting any significant lessons learned, achievements reached, painful moments endured, or obstacles overcome. Also, include your feelings about those occurrences as you remember them. If you are a visual person, it might help to draw a timeline. Do not leave out any significant event.

The goal of this exercise is to help you uncover forgotten material from your youth. This material can be used to demonstrate a long-standing dedication to the legal field, or to demonstrate the kind of person you are by painting an image of yourself as a child. Many of the essayists in the examples found in Part Two used anecdotes from childhood to illustrate their points. Essayists 19 and 34, for example, both mention instances from their childhood that demonstrate their long-standing commitment to political activism. Two essayists (1 and 38) take a different approach by writing about having been teased in their childhood because of physical differences and how they overcame these adversities.

Although these essayists do it well, be cautioned in advance that relying too heavily on accomplishments or awards won far in your past can diminish the strength of your points. Law schools are more interested in what you have been doing in and since college than in what you accomplished, no matter how impressive, in high school.

Assess Your Accomplishments

Write down anything you are proud of having done, no matter how small or insignificant it might seem. Do not limit your achievements to your career. If you have overcome a difficult personal obstacle, be sure to mention this. If something is important to you, it can speak volumes about who you are and what makes you tick.

Some accomplishments will be obvious, such as any achievement that received public accolade or acknowledgment. Essayist 10 writes about being a University Scholar, for example, and Essayist 16 writes about being one of a small minority of Korean women to study and practice business. Others are less obvious; often the most defining moments of our lives are those we are inclined to dismiss. Essayist 25, for example, writes of his accomplishment of overcoming his fear of heights during a sailing expedition.

List Your Skills

Do an assessment of your skills that is similar to the one you did for your accomplishments. Cast your net broadly. Being able to draw connections between your unique skills and how they will make you a good lawyer is what will make you memorable. Think about the LSAT during this exercise. This test is designed to gauge certain quantifiable skills. Think of other skills that are not specifically tested, such as professionalism, and emphasize strengths in these areas. Begin by looking back at the last exercise and listing the skills that are highlighted by your accomplishments. When you have a list of words, start brainstorming on other ways in which you have demonstrated these skills in the last few years. Pretend that you are defending these skills in front of a panel of judges. Stop only when you have proven each point to the best of your ability.

Analyze Personality Traits

There is a fine and fuzzy line between skills and personality traits that can be used to your advantage. Almost any quality can be positioned as a skill or ability if the right examples are used to demonstrate it. If you had trouble listing and defending your skills in the last exercise, then shift the focus to your qualities and characteristics instead. Make a few columns on a sheet of paper. In the first column, list some adjectives you would use to describe yourself. In the next one, list the words your best friend would use. Use the other columns for the perceptions of people—perhaps one for your boss and another for family members or coworkers.

Now, see which words come up the most often. Look for such words as maturity, responsibility, sense of purpose, academic ability, intellectual curiosity, creativity, thoughtfulness, trustworthiness, sense of humor, perseverance, commitment, integrity, enthusiasm, confidence, conscientiousness, candor, leadership, goal-orientation, independence, and tact, to name a few. Group them together and list the different situations in which you have exhibited these characteristics. How effectively can you illustrate or prove that you possess all of these qualities? How do these qualities reflect on your ability to succeed in the world of law and politics?

Note Major Influences

You can refer back to your Top Ten lists for help getting started with this exercise. Was there a particular person who shaped your values and views? Did a particular book or quote make you rethink your life? Relationships can be good material for an essay, particularly a relationship that challenged you to look at people in a different way. Perhaps you had a wise and generous mentor from whom you learned a great deal. Have you had an experience that changed how you see the world, or defines who you are? What details of your life, special achievements and pivotal events have helped shape you and influence your goals?

Essayist 20 built his essay around the influence of a book he read in college. Notice, though, that the bulk of the essay is spent on himself and the changes that were manifested, rather than on the book itself. This is always the best approach when writing about an influence. Committees are not, after all, interested in learning about a fascinating person, character, or book—they are interested in learning about you.

Identify Your Goals

The first step of this exercise is to let loose and write down anything that comes to mind regarding your goals: What are your dreams? What did you want to be when you were younger? If you could do or be anything right now, regardless of skill, money, or other restrictions, what would it be? Think as broadly as you wish, and do not limit yourself to professional goals. Will you have children? What kind of house will you live in and what kinds of friends will you have?

The second step is to begin honing in on some more specific or realistic goals. Given your current skills, education, and experience, where could you expect to be in 20 years? Where would you be ideally? Think in terms of five-year increments, listing actual positions and places if possible. Be detailed and thorough in your assessment, and when you think you have finished, dig a little deeper. Are you drawn more to the interpretation of law, or to doling out justice, or in politics and public service? Make it clear in your own mind what becoming a lawyer means specifically to you. Make sure it is more than guaranteed income and getting to write "Esq." after your name.

You are not required (or even expected) to write about specific career goals in your essay, but you should still work through this exercise. You may think that your goals are obvious, but there is actually a wide range of career goals that a law degree will prepare you for, ranging from politics to litigation to teaching. When you can show the admissions committee that you have thought more specifically about your post-law school life it reemphasizes your sincerity. More importantly, though, goals are tied in very tightly with motivation. Brainstorming about your goals will clue you in better to your motivation—and unlike specific goals, specific motivation *is* something that you are expected to write about.

At this and every stage of brainstorming, do not hesitate to expand and modify lists that you created previously. If at this stage of the process you realize that a strong influence in your life was not in your original list, that doesn't mean it is any less important to you. Add it now. The subconscious mind has an interesting way of retrieving information like this, and the brainstorming process is meant to uncover as much of it as possible, in whatever way it surfaces.

Before You Move On

Knowing yourself, your motivations, and your goals thoroughly can be difficult. Not all of your motivations, significant influences, defining experiences, or career goals—especially long-term—are going to be completely clear to you at this point. However if these exercises proved more than a little difficult for you, it could be a sign that you need to step back and reassess your decision to apply. Because expressing your reasons for applying to law school is so central to the personal statement, giving vague reasons will indicate ambivalence to the committee, and that alone could ruin your chances of getting into law school.

Before you go any further, reassess your decision to attend law school. Look more closely into what having the degree will do for you and whether it will allow you to achieve what you truly want. If you are not clear yourself about exactly why you want it and what you will do once you have it, how will you be able to convince an admissions committee?

On the other hand, if this chapter was helpful to you, you should now have plenty of material—in fact, more than you need—to write successful and convincing essays. The next chapter, Develop a Strategy, will help you understand how to present this material as a cohesive whole, leaving the committee with a strong sense of who you are and a persuasive, targeted argument for why they should accept you.

CHAPTER 3

Develop a Strategy

Chapter Highlights

- A strong essay will include why you are applying to law school, how you are unique, and examples of your qualifications.
- Multiple themes should be woven together seamlessly.
- Alternative approaches to the personal statement should be attempted only by applicants with very strong GPAs and LSATs.

Do's and Don'ts

- Do demonstrate your motivations by providing evidence.
- Don't make unsubstantiated statements.
- Do express yourself through stories and personal accounts.
- Don't be trite or predictable.
- Do state how a law degree will enhance your career.
- Don't use legacy as a primary motivation.
- Do discuss your work experience.
- Don't make lists.
- Do discuss diversity with tact.
- Don't repeat data found elsewhere in your application.

At this stage you should have plenty of material from which to build your personal statement: You have a solid understanding of your motivations, goals, and qualifications—academically, professionally, and personally—and you have plenty of details to back them up. The details should comprise specific examples from your past, perhaps the summer spent grappling with legalese at a law firm, your volunteer experience setting up a model U.N., or the time you lobbied for the repeal of curfew laws as a teenager.

Now it is time to mesh these disparate details of your life into a cohesive whole. This chapter represents the final stage of preparation, and the last step you need to take before you begin to write the first draft of your essay. In it you will choose your themes and develop a strategy.

Choose Your Themes

Part of what makes the personal statement so difficult is that you need to do so much in one essay. Unlike the college application essay where your motivation is unquestioned and your goals can remain undefined, and unlike other graduate programs where you are expected to write multiple essays in response to specific questions, writing a personal statement for admission to law school requires that you incorporate multiple themes in one composition. Needless to say, this can be tricky.

There are three basic themes for you to consider:

1. Why you want to be a lawyer/attend this law school.

2. What makes you unique, different, or exceptional.

3. Why you are qualified.

You might focus on only one theme or try to incorporate all three. No matter how you choose to do it, remember that if your essay doesn't ultimately express your motivation for attending law school and pose an argument for why you should be accepted, you've missed the mark.

With that said, though, remember that it is the quality of the essay itself and not the choice of theme that determines the success or failure of a personal statement. For every theme there are people who do them well and people who simply do them.

My favorite essays are invariably the ones that demonstrate, with passion, why the candidate wants to be a lawyer. My least favorite essays are invariably the ones that demonstrate, with passion, why the candidate wants to be a lawyer.

The challenge of successfully incorporating these arguments into your statement is to do it in a way that still grabs the attention of the committee. Because all applicants are working to accomplish the same goal, the essays can start sounding very much the same. As was discussed in the first chapter, admissions officers can read up to 40 or 50 essays a day, so monotony quickly becomes their number one pet peeve. Below you will find some tips and advice to help you incorporate your themes while avoiding the pitfalls inherent in each.

Theme 1: Why I Want to Be a Lawyer

The secret to pulling off this theme is to demonstrate why you want to be a lawyer. Don't just say it and expect it to stand on its own. Admissions officers want believable details from your life that demonstrate your desire and make it real to them.

> *Although you do get tired of reading it, it's nearly impossible (and ill-advised!) for an applicant to avoid communicating at some point that: "I want to be a lawyer." It's the ones who say only that that rankle. The ones who support the statement with interesting and believable evidence are the ones who do it best.*

One secret to avoiding the here-we-go-again reaction is to keep an eye on your first line. Starting with "I've wanted to be a lawyer since . . ." makes admissions officers cringe. Yes, we know it's an easy line to fall back on, but these poor people have read this sentence more times than they can count, and it gets old fast. Instead, start with a story that demonstrates your early call to law. Look, for example, at the first paragraph of Essay 34:

> *"That's not fair." Even as the smallest of children, I remember making such a proclamation: in kindergarten it was "not fair" when I had to share my birthday with another little girl and didn't get to sit on the "birthday chair." When General Mills changed my favorite childhood breakfast cereal, "Kix," I, of course, thought this was "not fair." Unlike many kids (like my brother) who would probably have shut up and enjoyed the "great new taste" or switched to Cheerios, this kid sat her bottom down in a chair (boosted by the phone book) and typed a letter to the company expressing her preference for the "classic" Kix over the "great new taste" Kix.*

In telling the story, this writer demonstrates that the roots of her political activism run deep without having to ever say it. She doesn't just tell us and expect us to take her word for it—she shows us through stories stemming back to early childhood.

Another approach that is overdone is the "my dad is a lawyer" approach. Some admissions officers said that when the only reason an applicant gives for wanting to be a lawyer is that it is a family legacy, it makes them question not only the motivation but the maturity of the applicant. While this doesn't mean you need to hide the fact that your parent is a lawyer, it does mean that you should avoid depending on that as your sole reason for wanting to go to law school. If a parent truly was your inspiration, then describe exactly why you were inspired by them, and what you have done to test your motivation in the real world.

An interesting twist on the "why I want to be a lawyer" theme is "why a law degree will make me a better businessperson, politician, analyst, etc." If a law degree is a means to an end other than specifically practicing law, feel free to say so. But be forewarned: You must make an extremely compelling case as to why the law degree is essential to your ultimate career goals. If it is not clear that you could only achieve your goals with a law degree, the admissions committee is likely to question your motivation. If your desire in life is to get to "point B," and there are multiple ways to get you there, taking the path that leads through law school may not be the most direct. You must prove to the committee that you won't simply change your roadmap if and when law school proves to be a difficult path.

Theme 2: Why I Am Qualified

Writing about your experiences in the law field supports both the Why I Want to Be a Lawyer theme and the Why I Am Qualified theme, so it is always a good idea to spend time on the experiences that qualify you as a potential law student.

Direct work experience is always the best, of course, for a number of reasons. For one, it proves your dedication to the committee. For another, it shows that you have the potential for being successful in the field. Perhaps most importantly, it shows the committee that you understand the profession and know what you will be getting into upon graduating. One type of applicant that the committee keeps a wary eye out for is the kind who wants to go to law school but doesn't have any realistic idea of what lawyers do beyond the glamorized images seen in television and movies.

You do not need to have had an internship at a law firm to show that you are qualified. Your experience might be political, such as the convention you volunteered to help organize or the campaign for which you helped raise funds. It can also be academic or issues-based, such as the thesis you wrote on law and the Internet. The rule here is, if you have it, use it.

If you have a lot of experience, the bulk of your essay may be spent on this theme rather than on the Why I Want to Go to Law School theme. You should try to relate your qualifications back to your motivation at some point, though, even if it is only a reference. Often, people will do this in a single, concluding sentence. This can be a powerful approach as long as your passion is clearly demonstrated through your description of your experiences. Look at Essay 19 for an example of this. The writer spends all but the last paragraph of his essay describing his dedication to activism, first by lobbying to have the Confederate flag removed from the Boy Scouts, and later by actions taken as student body president. He doesn't make a verbal tie-in to his motivation until the last few sentences of his essay:

> *I sought practical improvements through independent thinking, perseverance, and tenacity in the face of fierce criticism. A legal education would give me tools to better use these abilities. I am not headed to law school on a mission, but I see law as an opportunity to contribute as we build our future.*

Admissions Officers' Pet Peeve: Making Lists

For some candidates the problem will not be that they don't have enough direct experience to write about; they have too much. The danger inherent in wanting to include all your experience is that space is limited and you can either end up with an essay that is too long, or one that consists of little more than a listing of your activities and accomplishments.

The essay should never be merely a prose form of a C.V. That's dry to read, and again, doesn't offer any additional information about the candidate.

It is all right to include all the experience you have had somewhere in your essay but keep it short and do it in the context of a story or a personal account using colorful details. After all, you can attach a resume that will list all your jobs and promotions. The essay has the much more important job of bringing these experiences to life.

Also, resist the hard-sell approach. The admissions officers at top schools read so many essays written by extremely qualified applicants that writing a self-serving "I did this, I did that" essay isn't going to wow them; it will simply make them yawn. You are much better off with a humble attitude. Let your experiences speak for themselves and focus on making your essay personal and interesting instead. Having someone objective read your essay before you send it in will help you discern the kind of impression you are making.

Theme 3: Why I Am Exceptional

If you are different in any sense of the word—if you are an older applicant, a member of a minority, a foreign applicant, an athlete or musician, disabled, or have an unusual academic or career background, use this angle to your advantage by showing what your unique background will bring to the school and to the practice of law. One interesting topic for foreign students, for example, might be to talk about how the education system differs in this country and why they are choosing it over a course of study in their own country and/or language.

Beware, however, that there are instances where playing the diversity card will backfire:

If you are a "student of diversity" then of course, use it. But don't harp on it for its own sake or think that being different by itself is enough to get you in—that will only make us feel manipulated and it can show that you didn't know how to take advantage of a good opportunity.

Only people with significant and documentable disabilities should bring them up in the essay. By that I mean not the current popular over-diagnosed disability du jour, which in my day was ADD.

The secret is to tie in your diversity strongly with your motivations or qualifications, or with what you can bring to the class. If you can't make a strong

24

tie-in, then you might simply make a brief mention of your exceptional trait, background, or talent instead of making it the focus. This can be a very effective approach because it shows that you have enough confidence in your qualifications and abilities to let them stand on their own. It is as though you are simply mentioning the fact that you are blind or a refugee from a war-torn land or a violin virtuoso to add shading to your already strong, colorful portrait.

Some applicants, however, will have the opposite problem and will feel uncomfortable stressing their differences. Career switchers or older applicants, for example, sometimes feel insecure about incorporating their experience into the essay, thinking that they will only draw attention to the fact that the bulk of their experience is in another field. If this sounds like you, remember that your past experience gives you a unique perspective and you can use your essay to turn this into an advantage instead of a liability. Or, alternately, you could stress the similarities instead of the differences and make your diverse job experiences relevant by drawing comparisons between the skills required in your current field and the ones that will be needed in law school. The writer of Essay 15 does this when he likens his teaching of the Talmud to the study of law; Essayist 11 draws multiple parallels between studying English literature and his experiences volunteering with the American Civil Liberties Union.

Issues-Based Essays

Issues-based essays come in many different forms. The best kind of issues-based essays are written by applicants who have a strong passion for a specific cause and can show why the cause is important to them and what actions they have taken to further it. If there is an issue that dominates your thoughts, studies, or activities, it is natural that this issue will also dominate your essay.

Essay 12, for example, begins: "I am an activist with a commitment to fighting for progressive causes through legislation, policy, and grassroots organizing." She continues to demonstrate that she has been an active advocate for citizens' right to sexuality education and health care on many fronts.

Essayist 30 also writes about a single issue but does not focus on her own political activity. Rather, she uses the essay to argue against the injustice that currently exists in the court system regarding the issue of gay rights. She then relates her points to her motivation in the last sentence with:

> *Through obtaining a law degree, I hope to join many others in the struggle for our rights and dignity, and strive within an imperfect court system toward the goal of greater equality within the law.*

Other issues-based essays focus more on analyzing all sides of the issue rather than taking a stand from one viewpoint. If you do this type of essay well, it will show the committee that you are a person of reason and logic who can make mature, educated decisions based on a thorough analysis of issues. It is not even necessary that you come to any final conclusions—just showing that you can see and analyze all sides of an argument has validity.

Essayist 8, for example, analyzes the issue of Latin American labor laws. She offers a nonstandard viewpoint based on her first-hand experience in the Peace Corps, but acknowledges the other side of the argument as well, without coming to any final conclusion:

> *How to balance these positive factors with the often exploitative and abusive methods of the factory managers, or how to control the problems of rural-urban migration are questions I am still investigating.*

The pitfall inherent in any of the above issues-based approaches is that applicants who write about their commitment to a social justice issue without backing it up with real evidence or experience risk appearing insincere. If your beliefs are genuine, you will be able to support them with clear evidence of your involvement in activities that demonstrate your commitment. One admissions officer had this comment:

> *Year after year hundreds of applicants swear by their altruistic motives, yet only 2% of all lawyers graduating in 1991 took jobs in the public sector, protecting the environment, fighting racial inequality, and crusading for rights for the homeless. The majority (over 60%) took jobs in private firms. After a time, you become skeptical.*

Weave Your Themes Together

Once you have decided on the various themes to include in your essay, the last step is to develop a strategy—or in other words, determine how you will weave your themes together. Here is some advice you do not get often: Don't think about this one too much. The nice thing about strategy is that it tends to fall into place by itself once you develop an outline and start writing, which is what Chapter 4 is all about. So what we offer here is no more than a couple of tips for you to consider, but not to worry too much about. In the end there really is no more we can tell you about strategy without knowing more about you personally.

Strategy Tip 1: Keep the School in Mind

Most students write generic personal statements that are then sent to every school. That's fine, and to a degree it is expected. But, then again—

> *It always impresses us when applicants have done their research and taken the time to demonstrate why they are a good fit for our particular school.*

Don't be lazy about this! If you are able to write individual essays for each school, then you can at least find out about the school's general reputation by scanning the guidebook and catalog. It is better, however, to research the faculty and familiarize yourself with a school's specific strengths.

Strategy Tip 2: Keep the Rest of Your Application in Mind

This can mean a couple of different things. One is that you should not be redundant. Don't use the essay to repeat what can be found elsewhere in the application. Don't repeat your GPA or your LSAT score, no matter how impressive. And again, do not provide a prose listing of your activities and accomplishments—not only is that dull, but it shows that you don't know how to take advantage of a good opportunity to showcase your soft skills.

Also, you can use your essay to explain any kinds of obvious questions that would arise after reading the rest of your application. Because GPAs and LSATs are so important to the application process, applicants who have fallen short in either area are often tempted to use the essay to provide excuses for their poor performances. This is not always ill advised. If there is an anomaly in your record, the committee will look to your essay for an explanation.

> *If there is a hole or gap that appears in another part of the application, we will look to the statement for an explanation. If one is not provided, we start guessing. Anything the candidate provides is bound to be better than what we hypothesize in its absence.*

If you plan to address a shortcoming, however, tread lightly. Applicants who do it best provide a brief and mature explanation of the lapse, then spend the rest of the essay focusing on their strengths in other areas. The problems come when the applicant tries to excuse a problem instead of explain it, or dwells too long on whatever the hardships were that caused the problem.

> *Explaining a bad grade or even a bad semester can be done with finesse. I would never give staying away from that as blanket advice. But, please, just don't whine while you're doing it.*

Some applicants, for example, try to excuse low LSATs by claiming that they are not good test takers. Well, we hate to break it to them, but law school is about taking tests. They are a large part of the curriculum and are proven predictors of academic success. So why would admitting flat out to being a bad tester ever be a good thing?

Alternative Approaches

No matter how stringent these rules regarding theme and strategy may seem, there will always be applicants who decide to toss it all to the wind and take a completely different approach. The writer of Essay 6, for example, incorporates none of the mentioned themes into her personal statement. She does not talk about her motivation or qualifications for attending law school. In fact, she doesn't even mention the word "law" once. She chose, instead, to focus her entire essay on telling the story of an experience she had with an illness in Kenya.

This is a risky approach, and one that is best taken by students with very strong backgrounds and solid writing skills. This applicant obviously felt confident that the rest of her application spoke well enough of her qualifications that she could focus entirely on the lesson her story taught her—and her gamble paid off. The benefit of her approach is that she paints a vivid and memorable picture of herself. She shows that she is determined and level-headed and has a good sense of humor.

Ultimately, it is a personal decision. Again, the best way to gauge whether or not the risk is one worth taking is by finding a reader capable of giving you objective and informed feedback.

CHAPTER 4

At Last, Write!

Chapter Highlights

- Creating an outline will help you write a well-structured essay.

- Properly constructed paragraphs are the pillars of the essay.

- Effective transitions between paragraphs are essential to a cohesive essay.

- The lead should grab your reader's attention from the beginning.

- The final sentence should tie together loose ends, summarize, or emphasis your main points.

Do's and Don'ts

- Don't overuse transitional words (however, nevertheless, furthermore).

- Do use a thesaurus if you are having trouble finding the right word.

- Don't overuse the thesaurus—it will show.

- Do choose verbs over adverbs and adjectives as much as possible.

- Don't use sentences that are excessively long or short.

Now that you know what you want your personal statement to say, it is time to start writing. First, set a time limit of no more than a couple of days. The longer your time frame, the more difficult it will be to write your first draft. The point is to not allow yourself to simply wait for inspiration to strike. As one admissions officer put it, "Some of the worst writing ever crafted has been done under the guise of inspiration."

Relieve some of the pressure of writing by reminding yourself that this is only a draft. Rid yourself of the notion that your essay can be perfect on the first try. Do not agonize over a particular word choice, or the phrasing of an idea; you will have plenty of time to perfect the essay later. For now, the most important thing is to *get the words on paper.*

Creating an Outline

You are probably familiar with the structure of the traditional outline taught in most elementary schools:

Paragraph 1
    Introduction that contains the central idea

Paragraph 2
    Topic sentence that ties into the central idea
    First supporting point
    Evidence for point

Paragraph 3
    Topic sentence that links the above paragraph to the next
    Second supporting point
    Evidence for point

Paragraph 4
    Topic sentence that links the above paragraph to the next
    Third supporting point
    Evidence for point

Paragraph 5
    Conclusion that reiterates the central idea and takes it one step further

This method is still your best bet. The problem is that it may not allow for the complexities of incorporating multiple themes into a personal statement. Your outline will probably need to be more elaborate than this one, but that is no excuse for not having one. In fact, the more complex the essay, the more it requires an outline. Without it, your essay will lack structure; without structure, your essay will be rambling and ineffective.

Take some time to play with the material you have, putting it into different structures, always with the goal of offering the best support for your main points. Look at some of the examples below to get ideas for different types of outlines:

Standard Structure

The standard structure is the most common and is recommended for use in almost any circumstance. It is as close as you will get to the simple structure outlined above. The general application of the standard structure is to introduce your themes and main points in the introduction, use the body of the text to supply a single supporting point per paragraph, and then reiterate your main points or draw a new conclusion in the last. The following is an example of a standard structure used by Essayist 12 who writes of her experience as a political activist:

Paragraph 1 (Introduction)

Leading Sentence: "I am an activist with a commitment to fighting for progressive causes through legislation, policy, and grassroots organizing."

Introduces Theme: She has been active in many political projects, but her main focus has been as an advocate for sexuality education and health care.

States Intent: "In this statement I will explain how I gained expertise in this field through both academic and professional work from 1988 to the present."

Paragraph 2

Transition/Topic Sentence: "At [Ivy League University] I began my commitment to reproductive health."

Point and Evidence: She was committed to reproductive health issues academically, as evidenced by her major in women's studies and legal issues, her study on the impact of the abortion pill on the National Health Service, and her thesis on the legal treatment of pregnant substance abusers.

Paragraph 3

Transition/Topic Sentence: "While I was a student, I gained professional experience as a birth control counselor at the University health clinic."

Point and Evidence: She was committed to reproductive health issues in her extracurricular activities as well, both as a counselor and as a Planned Parenthood educator.

Paragraph 4

Transition/Topic Sentence: "When I moved to a small desert town in the Western United States, I volunteered for a democratic congressional campaign, where I briefed the candidate on abortion rights and sexuality issues in health care reform."

Point and Evidence: Her first job experience involved health care activism, as the Director of Public Affairs at Planned Parenthood.

Paragraph 5

Transition/Topic Sentence: "I quickly learned that this small town was far more conservative than my university's eastern college community."

Point and Evidence: She dealt with opposition to her efforts by publishing articles and op-ed pieces based on her research of local right wing activists.

Paragraph 6

Transition/Topic Sentence: "When my State Senator asked me to manage his reelection campaign, I eagerly accepted since I knew he had worked hard in support of health care and civil rights."

Point and Evidence: She learned valuable lessons by creating effective political messages, managing volunteers, and so on.

Paragraph 7

Transition/Topic Sentence: "I had hoped to work in the state capitol after the campaign, and I am now working for a state level health care advocacy organization which employs a lobbyist and coordinates grassroots strategy."

Point and Evidence: She continues her dedication to health care and politics in her current position by researching legislation, helping the director, etc.

Paragraph 8 (Conclusion)

Transition/Topic Sentence: "While I believe that I have developed both academic and professional expertise in reproductive health policy, health care reform, and political organizing, I would like to acquire the skills and power to make a bigger difference."

Concluding Summary: The writer reiterates the main points and gives a tie-in with her motivation to attend law school and her goals after graduation.

Issue Analysis

Not everyone chooses the traditional standard structure for a personal statement. Some writers choose to focus their essays on the analysis of an issue or argument as the writer of Essay 8 did. She writes about the effects of development in Latin America, or more specifically, on women factory workers. Notice how her structure highlights the most crucial aspects of what she must accomplish: 1) she makes the issue personal, 2) she states her argument clearly using specific evidence to back it up, 3) she discusses both sides of the issue, 4) she shows how she has been active in promoting the issue in the real world, and, most importantly, 5) she relates her analysis of the issue to her motivation to attend law school.

Paragraph 1 (Introduction)

Leading sentence: "After college I served for two and a half years in Honduras with the U.S. Peace Corps."

Introduces theme: She introduces the theme of development in Latin America and makes it personal by relating it to her experience in Honduras.

States focus: "I found potential for changing some of the larger problems of development in a surprising arena, maquilardoras, or textile factories."

Paragraph 2

Transition/Topic Sentence: "While in Honduras I talked to many women who worked in maquilardoras."

Point and Evidence: She introduces her point of view that the factories are not as negative as is portrayed in academic teaching. She supports this with evidence taken from her first-hand experience in Honduras.

Paragraph 3

Transition/Topic Sentence: "The factory jobs had other positive side effects."

Point and Evidence: She provides more solid evidence for her argument by citing the workers' higher salaries and better education.

Paragraph 4

Transition/Topic Sentence: "How to balance these positive factors with the often exploitative and abusive methods of the factory managers, or how to control the problems of rural-urban migration are questions I am still investigating."

Point and Evidence: She steps back to examine other sides of the argument, but ends by restating her position.

Paragraph 5

> *Transition/Topic Sentence:* "With the new U.S. policy focus on trade with Latin America and with more and more businesses using labor abroad, labor conditions in maquiladoras will be a growing human rights issue."
>
> *Point and Evidence:* She addresses the relevance of the issue to the future, and gives evidence of actions she has taken to promote national discussion and exposure of the issue.

Paragraph 6 (Conclusion)

> *Transition/Topic Sentence:* "A law degree would give me a tool to continue to work effectively and realistically on this and other issues that contribute to the well-being of people affected by U.S. policies and investments in Latin America."
>
> *Point:* She relates her involvement and discussion of this issue to her motivation to attend law school.

Compare and Contrast

In lieu of having direct law experience, some applicants will instead draw parallels between the experience they do have and the skills required of law students. In this case they might choose the Compare and Contrast structure. This was used by the writer of Essay 15 who focused on the comparison between law school and the study of the Talmud. This structure can be used to illustrate a change in your life by contrasting who you were before the change compared to who you are now. Essayist 20 does this when talking about the influence that a book had on his approach to learning, as does Essayist 38 when talking about himself before and after his first semester of college.

Chronological

Another way to create an outline for your essay is to structure your points chronologically. You could, for instance, follow your life through the various stages of growth, beginning with yourself in childhood, moving to high school, then to college, and so on. The advantage of this approach is that it is inherently personal and helps the committee to learn about you and how you matured. The drawback is that it can be hard to maintain focus and keep the essay short—the points you want to make can get lost in the narration of your life.

The writer of Essay 3 uses a chronological structure after a standard introduction:

Paragraph 1 (Introduction)

> *Leading sentence:* "My background as an engineer and a Hispanic affords me a unique point of reference from which a constructive engagement in the intellectual, political, and social spheres at [   ] will be enhanced."

Paragraph 2

> *Begins at birth:* "I was born in Brazil and lived in Mexico City starting at the age of two."

Paragraph 3

> *Jumps to college:* "I pursued an education in engineering taking my Bachelor of Science in Aeronautics and Astronautics from MIT in 1990 . . ."

Paragraph 4

> *Shifts to graduate school:* "At Michigan, my outside interests gravitated toward politics."

Paragraph 5

> *Continues with first job:* "After graduating from Michigan I worked as an engineer for General Electric Aircraft Engines for two and a half years."

Paragraph 6

> *Continues to current job:* "I left GE because I was dissatisfied with the opportunity for career growth . . ."

Paragraph 7

> *Brings us to present day:* I was immediately given the duties normally associated with a first or second year associate at a large firm."

Paragraph 8: (Conclusion):

> *Concluding sentence:* "I firmly believe my experiences in law, engineering, civic activity, and political activism will allow me to be a creative and contributing member of the intellectual life at . . ."

Incorporating the Narrative

Incorporating a story into your essay is a common and effective method for catching and keeping the reader's interest. It is also a good approach if you want to focus your essay around a single event in your life.

The most common way to incorporate the narrative into the personal statement is to begin by telling the story, then step out into the role of narrator to make points and draw conclusions.

The following are some examples of writers who have incorporated narrative into their essays. Notice how each writer steps out of the narrative at some point to discuss how the story relates to his or her motivations, goals, or qualifications for attending law school:

Essay 21: Tells the story of attending a Republican Convention as a (self-described) moderately liberal black man.

Essay 25: The writer tells the story of overcoming a fear of heights by joining a ship's crew one summer.

Essay 27: This essayist begins with the story of having to dole out punishments to two soldiers in his battery.

Essay 28: Begins with two separate stories, one of teaching English to refugees in Central America, another of trying to recruit a worker into the Steelworkers' Union.

Notice the variety of structures this type of essay can have and the number of situations that can be used. A narrative can span a lifetime or a moment. It does not have to be filled with Hollywood-style action to hold interest. The briefest and simplest event can have significance when told effectively. What makes all of these essays effective is their use of detail, description, and momentum.

Pure Narrative

In its purest form, a narrative essay does nothing but tell a story—it begins and ends with the action. This is not generally recommended for a personal statement because at some point the connection needs to be drawn from the story to your motivation and qualifications for attending law school, but there are some who pull it off well. The writer of Essay 6 is one of them. She tells the story of being treated for an illness in Kenya. She begins with action:

> *I was released from the Lamu hospital on a Monday morning.*

And ends with action:

> *With those words, she left me with a bill for twenty dollars, some salty greens to chew on twice a day, and a prescription for life.*

It is good to note, though, that the ones who can best execute this type of risky approach are those whose records (grades, scores, and experience) speak for themselves. If you are confident about the rest of your application, and you are an accomplished writer, writing a story for your essay will certainly catch the committee's eye and make you a more memorable candidate.

Paragraphs

Paragraphs are the pillars of the essay; they uphold and support the structure. Each one that you write should express a single thought and contain a clearly defined beginning, middle, and end. The examples of essay structures outlined above are also good examples of essays with strong paragraphs. The flow and points of the essays can be followed simply by reading the first sentences of each. Also notice how each paragraph supports only one point and expresses a single idea that is backed up with evidence. This is true whether the essay is following a formal standard structure or is focused on telling a story or the chronology of a life.

Transitions

We have demonstrated that the first sentence of every paragraph is extremely important. Collectively, they uphold the structure of your essay and help create strong, targeted paragraphs, but most importantly, they serve as transitions linking your points together. An essay without good transitions is like a series of isolated islands: The reader will struggle to get from one point to the next. Use transitions as bridges between your ideas.

The transition into the final paragraph is especially critical. If it is not clear how you arrived at this final idea, you have either shoehorned a conclusion into the outline, or your outline lacks focus. You should not have to think too much about consciously constructing transitional sentences. If the concepts in your outline follow and build on one another naturally, transitions will practically write themselves. To make sure that you are not forcing them, try to limit the use of such words as: *however, nevertheless,* and *furthermore.*

If you are having trouble transitioning between paragraphs or are trying to force a transition into a paragraph that has already been written, it may be indicative of a problem with your structure. If you suspect this to be the case, go back to your original outline and make sure that you have assigned only one point to each paragraph, and that each point naturally follows the preceding one and leads to a logical conclusion. This may result in a "back to the drawing board" restructuring effort, but try not to get discouraged. This happens to even the most seasoned writers and is a normal part of the writing process.

Word Choice

Well-structured outlines, paragraphs, and transitions are all an important part of a creating a solid essay—but structure isn't everything. An essay can be very well organized with balanced paragraphs and smooth transitions and still come across as dull and uninspired. You know from Chapter 1 that details are an integral part of interesting essays. Adding detail is certainly a good start, but there is more to know about the kind of writing that holds a reader's attention. First, there is word choice.

Rule 1: Put your thesaurus away

It will not make you look smarter; it will only make you look as if you are *trying* to look smarter.

Rule 2: Focus on verbs

Keep adjectives to a minimum. Pumping your sentences full of adjectives and adverbs is not the same as adding detail or color. Adjectives and adverbs add description, but verbs add action—and action is always more interesting than description.

One of the admissions officers on our panel advises using the following test to gauge the strength of your word choice:

The Verb Test

Choose a paragraph from your essay and make a list of every verb you have used. Compare your list to one of the following, taken from essays that were not used in this book:

COLUMN 1	COLUMN 2
said	has me
contorted	can say
complain	know
learned	are usually
spreading	may have heard
sprang	are
strained	is
gripped	strive
had been living	may not be involved
had attended	try to perform

If you had to choose an essay based solely on the verb list, which one would you rather read? Which list does yours more closely resemble?

Sentence Length and Structure

Another way to analyze the strength of your writing is to examine the pacing of your sentences. This is a good time to read your essay out loud. As you read, listen to the rhythm of the sentences. Are they all the same length? If each of your sentences twists and turns for an entire paragraph, try breaking them up for variety. Remember that short sentences have great impact.

One way to determine whether you are using a variety of different sentence lengths is to put S, M, or L (for short, medium, and long) above each sentence in a paragraph. A dull paragraph can look something like this:

M M M L M S S S M L

On the other hand, an interesting paragraph may look more like this:

S L M M L S

Beginnings and Endings

Beginnings and endings can be the most challenging parts of crafting any piece of writing, and also, in many ways, the most important. One of the reason they are so difficult is that writers tend to worry about them too much. There is much focus on the necessity of thoroughly introducing the subject and ending with sharply drawn conclusions that anxious essayists compensate by going overboard. They feel that in order to appear mature and worldly, their essays must contain profound insights and grand observations.

Do not fall into this trap! One of the biggest complaints from our admissions officers was that essayists tried to say and do too much in their introductions. "Just tell the story!" was their collective response to essayists who were trying too hard to impress. Many of these essays (not included in this book) would have been vastly improved had they simply removed their introductions altogether.

What? No Introduction?

Do yourself a favor and forget about beginnings and endings during the first stages of writing. Dive straight into the body of the text without bothering to introduce your themes or set the scene. The reason this technique works is that when you have finished writing the rest of your rough draft, you may discover that you do not need an introduction at all. This may be risky, but believe it or not, more essays have been ruined by forced and unnecessary introductions than have been ruined by the lack of one: This is largely due to the misconception of what an introduction is supposed to accomplish.

This is especially true if you are basing your essay around a story. You might believe it is risky or uncomfortable to allow the story to stand on its own without first being introduced, but beginning with action is always a good idea as long as the action is tied closely to the points you are trying to make throughout the rest of the essay.

Leading the Way

The most important part of any beginning is, of course, the lead. Leads play the dual role of setting the theme of your essay and engaging the reader. The introduction should not be overly formal or stilted. You do not want an admissions officer to start reading your essay and think, "here we go again." Although admissions officers will try to give the entire essay a fair reading, they are only human—if you fail to capture their interest after the first sentence, the rest of your essay will not get the attention it deserves.

Just as you should not worry about your introduction until you have an initial draft on paper, you should not begin by writing your lead unless you are feeling inspired about a particular line. Often, you will spot a good lead floating around in the middle of your first draft of the essay, so do not waste time worrying about it until you have the bulk of your essay on paper.

There are many different kinds of effective leads, some examples of which are listed below.

Standard Lead

Standard leads are the most common leads used. A typical standard lead answers one or more of the six basic questions: *who, what, when, where, why* and *how*. They give the reader an idea of what to expect. A summary lead is a kind of standard lead that answers most of these questions in one sentence. The problem with this kind of lead is that, although it is a logical beginning, it can be dull. The advantage is that it sets your reader up for a focused and well-structured essay. If your essay lives up to that expectation, the impact of your points is heightened. They are also useful for shorter essays when you need to get to the point quickly. The following are some examples of standard leads.

> *My background as an engineer and a Hispanic affords me a unique point of reference from which a constructive engagement in the intellectual, political, and social spheres at [school] will be enhanced.* (Essay 3)

> *To study law in [an] American law school is the intersection of three sets composing my life: my belief in international trade, my interest in establishing international trade law based on economic principles, and the contribution that I can make as a Korean woman.* (Essay 16)

> *While my undergraduate record and letters of recommendation are informative about my capacity to succeed academically in law school, I intend the following statement to reveal something about the kind of lawyer I plan to become: thoughtful, ethically oriented, and capable of developing my ideas through personal experience.* (Essay 26)

Action Lead

This lead takes the reader into the middle of a piece of action. It is perfect for short essays where space needs to be conserved or for narrative essays that begin with a story.

> *When the federal agents arrived early that morning, my friend Adam didn't have a chance.* (Essay 17)

> *The wind shook my tent and drove the rain hard against the canvas.* (Essay 27)

> *When I was five years old, my family fled our homeland, the war-torn country of Vietnam.* (Essay 31)

Personal or Revealing Lead

This lead reveals something about the writer. It is always written in the first person and usually takes an informal, conversational tone:

> *I met my great-grandmother through her diaries.* (Essay 4)

> *When I began my freshman year at [school], I did not expect that five years later I would find myself documenting a massacre in a guerrilla-controlled area of El Salvador and establishing a school there for refugees who had recently returned to their country.* (Essay 33)

Creative Lead

These leads, when executed well, are more interesting by being obtuse or funny. They can leave you wondering what the essay will be about, or make you smile:

People often refer to a "body of law" but to me the most interesting limbs are the legs. (Essay 2)

What the hell am I doing? (Essay 21)

June 1987. (Essay 28)

Quotation Lead

This type of lead can be a direct quotation or a paraphrase. It is most effective when the quote you choose is unusual, funny, or obscure, and not too long. Choose a quote with a meaning you plan to reveal to the reader as the essay progresses. Some admissions officers caution against using this kind of lead because it can seem that you are trying to impress them. Do not use a proverb or cliché without good reason, and do not interpret the quote in your essay. The admissions committee is more interested in how you respond to it and what that response says about you:

You can't judge a book by its cover. (Essay 1)

How many a man has dated a new era in his life from the reading of a book. —Thoreau (Essay 20)

Dialogue Lead

This lead takes the reader into a conversation. It can take the form of an actual dialogue between two people or can simply be a snippet of personal thought:

"Where did we go wrong" were the first words offered by my mechanical engineering professor when I told him I wanted to go to law school. (Essay 24)

"That's not fair." (Essay 34)

Fact Lead

This lead gives the reader a fact or a statistic that is connected to the topic of the essay or simply provides a piece of information about the writer or a situation:

In December of 1988, Texas state District Court Judge Jack Hampton sentenced a man convicted of double homicide to a term of thirty years. (Essay 30)

Many people criticize required college courses and what others study as being useless in the real world. (Essay 7)

Closing Your Case

The final sentence of your essay is also critical. It must finish your thought or assertion, and it is an important part of creating a positive and memorable image. Endings are the last experience an admissions officer has with your essay, so you need to make those words and thoughts count.

The most common close used in personal statements is the standard close. The standard close either summarizes the main points of the essay or asserts (or reasserts) the writer's desire or qualification to attend law school. Some examples of standard closes include:

I firmly believe my experiences in law, engineering, civic activity, and political activism will allow me to be a creative and contributing member of the intellectual life at [school]. Thank you for your consideration. (Essay 4)

Your consideration of my application is in all reality a review of my efforts to fulfill my four-year, two-fold plan. I hope you find, as I believe, that I come well-prepared. (Essay 10)

I have the capability, the perspective, and the commitment to become a lawyer; I am prepared to take on the social and civic duties that this vocation demands. (Essay 13)

Through obtaining a law degree, I hope to join many others in the struggle for our rights and dignity, and strive within an imperfect court system toward the goal of greater equality within the law. (Essay 30)

If you have introduced a clever or unusual thought or image in the first paragraph, try referring back to it in your conclusion. The aim is for the admissions officer to finish your essay thinking, "That was a satisfying read," and "I wish there were more."

Essay 29, for example, closes with:

If I were to write an article on myself, it would be one of overcoming self-inflicted personal adversity, becoming the person I always knew I could be, and ending with a successful first year of law school.

This writer's reference to writing an article on himself relates back to his opening paragraph about the way his life might look through objective eyes. By referring back to this in his close, he wraps the essay up nicely and shows that time was spent in planning and structuring.

Essayist 22 also does this, and then ads an extra touch by ending his final sentence in a question relating back to his introduction about his decision to decline the opportunity of graduating two years early:

I would not trade those years for any "jump-start" on my career. Besides, who would really want to hire a 22-year-old lawyer anyway?

Adding a bit of humor at the end was a nice way for him to show the committee that he does not take himself as seriously as the rest of the essay might indicate. It plays the crucial role of humanizing him and making his essay personal.

Take a Break

You have made it through the first draft, and you deserve a reward for the hard work—take a break. Let your essay sit for a couple of days. You need to distance yourself from the piece so you can gain objectivity. Writing can be an emotional and exhausting process, particularly when you write about yourself and your experiences. After you finish your first draft, you may think a bit too highly of your efforts—or you may be too harsh. Both extremes are probably inaccurate. Once you have let your work sit for a while you will be better able to take the next (and final!) step presented in Chapter 5: Make It Perfect.

CHAPTER FIVE

Make It Perfect

Chapter Highlights

- It is constructive to take a break from your essay before beginning the first revision.
- The first revision should focus on content and structure.
- Reading aloud to detect awkward language or phrasing can be effective.
- Grammatical and spelling errors are unacceptable.

Writing is not a one-time act. Writing is a process, and memorable writing comes more from rewriting than it does from the first draft. By rewriting, you will improve your essay—guaranteed. There is no perfect number of drafts that will ensure a great essay, but you will eventually reach a point when your confidence in the strength of your writing is reinforced by the thoughts of others. If you skimp on the rewriting process, you significantly reduce the chances that your essay will be as good as it can be. Do not take that chance. The following steps show you how to take your essay from rough to remarkable.

Revise

Once you have taken a break away from your essay, come back and read it with a fresh perspective. Analyze it as objectively as possible based on the following three components: substance, structure, and interest. Do not worry yet about surface errors and spelling mistakes; focus instead on the larger issues. Be prepared to find some significant problems with your essays and be willing to address them even though it might mean significantly more work. Also, if you find yourself unable to smooth out the problems that turn up, you should be willing to start one or two of your essays from scratch, potentially with a new topic.

Substance

Substance refers to the content of your essay and the message you are sending out. It can be very hard to gauge in your own writing. One good way to make sure that you are saying what you think you are saying is to write down, briefly and in your own words, the message you are trying to communicate. Then remove the introduction and conclusion from your essay and have an objective reader review what is left and do the same. Compare the two statements to see how similar they are. This can be especially helpful if you wrote a narrative, to make sure that your points are being communicated in the story.

Here are some more questions to ask yourself regarding content:

- Have you answered the question that was asked?

- Is each point that you make backed up by an example?

- Are your examples concrete and personal?

- Have you been specific? Go on a hunt for generalities. Turn the generalities into specifics.

- Is the essay about you? (The answer should be "Yes!")

- What does it say about you? Try making a list of all the words you have used to describe yourself (directly or indirectly). Does the list accurately represent you?

- Does the writing sound like you? Is it personal and informal rather than uptight or stiff?

- Read your introduction. Is it personal and written in your own voice? If it is general or makes any broad claims, have someone proofread your essay once without it. Did the reader notice that it was missing? If the essay can stand on its own without it, then consider removing it permanently.

Structure

To check the overall structure of your essay, do a first-sentence check. Write down the first sentence of every paragraph in order. Read through them one after another, and ask yourself the following:

- Would someone who was reading only these sentences still understand exactly what you are trying to say?

- Are all of your main points expressed in the first sentences?

- Do the thoughts flow naturally, or do they seem to skip around or sound out of context?

Now go back to your essay as a whole and ask yourself:

- Does each paragraph stick to the thought that was introduced in the first sentence?

- Is each point supported by a piece of evidence? How well does the evidence support the point?

- Is each paragraph roughly the same length? When you step back and squint at your essay, do the paragraphs look balanced on the page? If one is significantly longer than the rest, you are probably trying to squeeze more than one thought into it.

- Does your conclusion draw naturally from the previous paragraphs?

- Have you varied the length and structure of your sentences?

Interest

Many people think only of mechanics when they revise and rewrite their compositions, but making your statement interesting is crucial in order to keep the admissions officers reading. Make your essay memorable. Look at your essay with the interest equation in mind: personal + specific = interesting. Answer the following:

- Is the opening paragraph personal? Do you start with action or an image?

- At what point does your essay really begin? Try to delete all the sentences before that point.

- Does the essay "show" rather than "tell"? Use details whenever possible to create images.

- Did you use any words that you would not use in a conversation? Did you take any words from a thesaurus? (If either answer is yes, get rid of them.)

- Have you used an active voice? (See more under The Hunt for Red Flags, below.)

- Did you do the verb check (see Chapter 4)? Are your verbs active and interesting?

- Have you overused adjectives and adverbs?

- Have you eliminated trite expressions and clichés?

- Does it sound interesting to you? If it bores you, it will bore others.

- Will the ending give the reader a sense of completeness? Does the last sentence sound like the last sentence?

The Hunt for Red Flags

How can you know if you are writing in a passive or active voice? Certain words and phrases are red flags for the passive voice, and relying on them too heavily will considerably weaken an otherwise good essay. To find out if your essay suffers from passivity, go on a hunt for all of the following, highlighting each one as you find it:

really	rather
there is	it is important to note that
it is essential that	however
nonetheless/nevertheless	in addition
in conclusion	for instance
yet	very
although	in fact
I feel	I believe
I hope	can be
maybe	perhaps
usually	may/may not
have had	somewhat

How much of your essay is highlighted? You do not need to eliminate these phrases completely, but ask yourself if each one is necessary. Try replacing the phrase with a stronger one. At times, particularly when writing about a subjective topic, the passive voice can be appropriate. It can cushion the way you describe a personal belief so as not to seem rigid in your thinking, or brash in your assertions. To help determine "how much is OK," use the Read Out Loud technique described below to guide you. In speech, you will likely hear passive phrasing reduce the impact of your statements, and can turn your assertions into mere suggestions. Used excessively, passive speech can weaken the overall credibility of what you are trying to convey.

Proofread

When you are satisfied with the structure and content of your essay, it is time to check for grammar, spelling, typos, and so on. There will be obvious things you can fix right away, such as a misspelled or misused word, a seemingly endless sentence, or improper punctuation. Keep rewriting until your words say what you want them to say. Ask yourself these questions:

- Did I punctuate correctly?

- Did I eliminate exclamation points (except in dialogue)?

- Did I use capitalization clearly and consistently?

- Did the subjects agree in number with the verbs?

- Did I place the periods and commas inside the quotation marks?

- Did I keep contractions to a minimum? Are apostrophes in the right places?

- Did I replace the name of the proper school for each new application?

Read Out Loud

To help you polish the essay even further, read it out loud. You will be amazed at the faulty grammar and awkward language that your ears can detect. It will also give you a good sense of the flow of the piece and will alert you to anything that sounds too abrupt or out of place. Good writing, like good music, has a certain rhythm. How does your essay sound? Interesting and varied, or drawn out and monotonous? Reading out loud is also a good way to catch errors that your eyes might otherwise skim over while reading silently.

Get Feedback

We have mentioned this point many times throughout this book, but it can never be emphasized enough: *Get feedback*! Not only will it help you see your essay objectively, it is also a good way to become reinspired when you feel yourself burning out.

You should have already found someone to proofread for general style, structure, and content as was advised in Chapter 1. If you have to write multiple essays for one school, have that person evaluate the set as a whole. As a final step before submitting your application, find someone new to proofread for the surface errors with fresh eyes.

As was said earlier, if you are having trouble finding someone willing (and able) to dedicate the time and thought that is needed to make this step effective, you may want to consider getting a professional evaluation. In addition to our own web site (www.ivyessays.com), a number of qualified services can be found on the Internet.

PART TWO

The Essays

This section contains more than 40 personal statements written by candidates who were accepted into top law schools in the United States. After each essay you will find comments written by the authors of this book. All typos, as well as grammatical and spelling errors found in the original essays, have been preserved. The only changes made were the elimination of personal information where requested by the applicant. Personal information (names of schools or places of employment, for example) that has been given a generic replacement is presented in brackets.

Despite the occasional surface errors, the essays were written by some of the most qualified applicants in the world and the quality of the essays is, on the whole, very good. However, we do not present these essays to you, as examples of works of perfection, we are in the business of helping our clients write the best possible essays. So while these essays were good enough to get each and every applicant into the law school of his or her choice, we reviewed them carefully and critically and found areas in which all but a few could be improved. In many cases, we focused more on improvements than on the essay's strengths so that our readers would potentially gain more valuable lessons from these examples.

To help you sort quickly through the statements that are most relevant to you, topic tags have been added to the top of each essay. Also, there is a cross-referenced Essay Index located at the end of this section that identifies essays by theme, subject, and the applicant's experience and background.

Among the schools to which these essayists were accepted are Harvard Law School, Stanford Law School, University of Chicago Law School, Cornell Law School, Boalt Hall Law School (UC Berkeley), New York University Law School, University of Virginia School of Law, University of Michigan Law School, Georgetown University Law Center, Columbia University School of Law, Duke University School of Law, University of North Carolina at Chapel Hill School of Law, and University of Pennsylvania Law School.

Please note that plagiarizing from these or any work that is not your own is illegal. Because IvyEssays works with admissions officers from schools around the country, the committees are familiar with many of the essays presented in this book. Use them as a learning tool and as a source of inspiration.

ESSAY 1: Overcoming a Childhood Obstacle; Legal Assistant; Senator's Office Staff Worker

"You can't judge a book by its cover." As a child, this was one cliché to which I was particularly devoted. In addition to the customary difficulties of adjusting to adolescence and a new school environment, I entered middle school with an unusual liability: I suffered from facial tics, the most persistent of which was a frequent, involuntary eye twitch. Only a few weeks into the seventh grade, I acquired the nickname "Blinky" and, at an age when insecurities already run rampant, my identity was permanently defined by the feature which I hated most in myself. Even back then I realized that the teasing was always affectionate, and I made friends quickly; nevertheless, I spent years with a nagging feeling that I was somehow aberrant. Gradually, however, my tics diminished in both frequency and intensity, and by the time I entered college they had largely disappeared.

I wanted to discuss this condition because I believe that, as an ever-present factor during many of these formative years, the experience played a major role in shaping the adult I have become. Although ten years ago I would never have foreseen that my tics could be a powerful vehicle for personal growth, I believe that the experience has helped me to develop a heightened sensitivity for those who have struggled to fit in socially. It was this factor, for example, which led me to become a Resident Assistant as an undergraduate at Stanford for two years, and which has prompted my involvement with various community service projects, giving me the opportunity to interact with troubled and disadvantaged youth.

Most importantly, as a person who often felt different while growing up—and who desperately wanted the other kids to judge the content of the book, rather than the quality of the cover—I have always made an effort in both my personal and in my professional life to scratch well beneath the surface, to determine whether the substance actually matches the form. My decision to attend law school also reflects this tendency. Although I have long had an interest in the law as an academic discipline, my work experience since graduating has given me the opportunity to confirm that my academic interests would extend to the real-world application of legal principles. To this end, I purposefully chose jobs that provided two very distinct perspectives on the practice of law: as a legal assistant, I became acquainted with both the advantages and disadvantages of private practice, while my current position in Senator X's office has offered a glimpse of how the law may be used constructively in the public sector. Although my own long-term goals are geared more towards the latter, both positions have equally impressed upon me the unique potential which exists in the law to make a direct, positive impact on people's lives.

Working for the law firm, I was initially turned off by the formal language which permeated all writing and discourse ("Aforementioned legalese had heretofore proven incomprehensible"). As one not familiar with the jargon, I found the law to be pretentious and distant. Gradually, however, I began to sort out the shades of difference between a "motion in limine" and a "56(f) motion," and I came to understand the law as a vast set of rules which could, with intelligence and creativity, genuinely be used on behalf of values such as fairness and justice. In addition to my primary assignment on an antitrust case, some exposure to pro bono work further convinced me that the law has a very important role to play in our society.

Similarly, my first impressions of Capitol Hill were not altogether favorable. Not only did I struggle to negotiate my way through the labyrinth of underground tunnels in order to find the cafeteria, but I was again forced to adapt to a specialized language, this time the unique lexicon of lobbyists and congressional staffers. As with my experience at the law firm, though, I soon realized the practical application of the laws which are written here in Congress. Unlike most of the general public, who see only the final version of a bill, being part of the legislative process has forced me to examine all sides of any given issue. Although politics can make this process agonizingly slow and inefficient, my work here has given me a greater appreciation for the way that laws affect our constituents back home.

Given my own particular skills and abilities, I am now convinced that the law presents the single greatest chance for me to make a difference, both in the lives of individuals and in terms of influencing the broader fabric of society. I am confident that my insistence on looking beyond those first impressions has provided me with an exciting opportunity, just as I would like to think that those seventh graders who eventually managed to look beyond an awkward physical trait also discovered something worthwhile.

Strengths

Beginning the essay with a quote sparks immediate interest. Discussing her childhood tics adds a very personal touch to the essay and makes the applicant seem humble and likeable. The author makes great use of her work experience to demonstrate a commitment to the field. The quote in the beginning is tied in and made even more relevant by the closing statement.

Weaknesses

The introductions in paragraphs 2 and 3 are overdone. Paragraph 2 would have been smoother simply beginning, "I believe that . . ." Paragraph 3 would have been better beginning, "As a person who often felt different . . ." Some sentences were too long. The final paragraph should be constructed from more than two sentences.

ESSAY 2: Interest in Public Policy; Health Care Experience

People often refer to a "body of law" but to me the most interesting limbs are the legs. Every law has legs. In other words, laws are constructed and structured within a certain historical moment shaped by particular social, economic, and political circumstances. Yet, laws must walk forward with time and be applied and interpreted within social contexts that did not exist when they were first created. It is the distance covered between a law's birth and its implementation and interpretation that interests me.

The creation of new law and the application of existing law to new circumstances are prisms to understanding our society and, perhaps, to changing it. There are many well-known examples of such transformative laws, including the CIvil Rights Act, the 19th Amendment, and the Roe v. Wade decision. From an intellectual perspective, I am interested in the historical forces and social context which are the underpinnings of any new law and therefore act as reflections of our society. For a more practical application, I am interested in how public policies can be structured to create social and economic opportunities and to foster equality. By pursuing a legal career, I feel that I am positioning myself to help shape, define, and implement such policies.

My undergraduate academic work focused on political economy and cultural identity. I was interested in understanding the forces behind the social, economic, and political structure of American society and the process by which people create their identities within this structure while changing it. The Residential College at the University of Michigan did not only provide a supportive environment to pursue these intellectual interests but also ensured that I acquired the skills to transfer my academic interests to a professional setting. Our professors challenged their students to conduct research, write analytical essays, engage in class debates, and make presentations. This experience prepared me well for the real world where the ability to write well, analyze precisely, facilitate discussions, and speak persuasively are essential skills. It also gave me the intellectual background and skills to move successfully into my first job as a research assistant at the Robert Wood Johnson Foundation where my interest in public policy was concentrated in health care policy development.

The Foundation's mission is to further social change with the specific goal of improving the health and health care of all Americans. Although I learned a lot about the theory, politics, and practical considerations involved in health care policy development and implementation at the

Foundation, I also realized that it is very difficult to affect public policy when you are removed from public institutions of government.

After moving to Denver, I applied for a position with the Colorado Department of Health Care Policy and Financing's Office of Public and Private Initiatives (OPPI) which is charged with health care policy development for the state. There were no openings at the time which initially disappointed me. However, I decided to use my time to sharpen my skills while exploring other aspects of the health care industry. I became an independent health care consultant.

Working for myself tested my initiative, responsibility, and analytical skills while giving me an opportunity to explore different kinds of work. I had to convince potential clients to trust my abilities despite my youth. Within the first three months of being self-employed, I had acquired three clients—a large Denver hospital, a health care publishing firm, and OPPI. Every time I see an ad for the Rose Sports Medicine Center, I am proudly reminded that I wrote the original business plan for the Center. Similarly, I am always gratified to find references to the fact book on physician groups that I helped develop and write at the publishing firm or when people call OPPI for a copy of my report on public opinion about health care in Colorado. I believe that none of my clients would have given the responsibility for the projects I completed to someone within their organizations with my level of experience. Because of my confidence in my ability to do the work and the independence I demonstrated in my approach to finding work, these organizations trusted me to complete projects important to them. Working in a variety of health care settings confirmed for me that my strongest interests are public policy and the law. Therefore, when I was offered a full-time position in OPPI, I felt that it was a great opportunity.

My interest in how law structures our society and reflects its changing values has been strengthened by the real life experience of developing public policy at the state-level. Attending law school is a logical continuation of the interests that I have pursued since college. Law school will provide insight into the theory and structure of the legal system as well as the historical and social journeys that laws travel from their conception to application. I intend to draw upon my practical experience in public policy and my legal education to guide my future efforts to help develop effective public policies.

Strengths

The author's interest in law and society is well documented by the work experience he discusses. He comes across as a confident and competent, self-starter, while never sounding arrogant. He accomplishes this especially well in paragraph 6.

Weaknesses

The analogy of law to a body with "legs" is a stretch and one that was not explained with great success. The essay is a bit dry and while the author's experience, motivation, and qualifications are well documented, they are not unveiled in an essay that is particularly enjoyable to read.

ESSAY 3: Career Switcher; Engineer; Hispanic; Athlete; Paralegal

My background as an engineer and a Hispanic affords me a unique point of reference from which a constructive engagement in the intellectual, political, and social spheres at [school] will be enhanced.

I was born in Brazil and lived in Mexico City starting at the age of two. When I was ten, my family moved to a small rural town in southwestern Michigan.

I am half Mexican and half German, born to parents whose families maintain close ties to Germany and Mexico. The rich mixture of cultures coupled with my own experiences living outside the US have allowed me to perceive the actions of the United States from a different perspective than that of many US citizens.

I pursued an education in engineering taking my Bachelor of Science in Aeronautics and Astronautics from [school] in 1990 and my Master of Science in Aerospace Engineering from [school], where I was a Merit Scholar Fellow, in 1991. I am proud that success at [school] was both academic and athletic. I maintained an above average GPA and participated in intercollegiate varsity water polo and swimming. Honored as captain of both teams, I also achieved a personal dream by earning All-America honors in my senior year.

At [school], my outside interests gravitated toward politics. My brother and sister were both heavily involved in the campus debates regarding political correctness, womens' issues, and race and class issues. My interest in the political and intellectual arena remains keen. I consider myself a principled and thoughtful advocate of progressive politics and, to the extent that time allows, I expect to be an active member of groups with similar political interests.

After graduating from [school] I worked as an engineer for General Electric Aircraft Engines for two and a half years. During this time, I completed a rigorous nine month in-house engineering curriculum (a joint program with Boston University) earning A's in both semesters. While at GE, I organized a voter registration drive that allowed 425 employees to register without having to leave work. This experience allowed me to work with senior executives of the Company and the Union while gaining an appreciation for the obstacles involved in getting both parties to work together, even for neutral goals.

I left GE because I was dissatisfied with the opportunity for career growth and a feeling that my efforts and those of my peers were neither recognized nor rewarded appropriately. My interest in social issues prompted me to explore a career in law.

Rather than apply directly to law school I obtained a job as a paralegal with a small corporate litigation firm in Manhattan. I wanted to experience law from the inside and the firm needed a turbine expert to act as a technical consultant during discovery, depositions, and arbitration.

I was immediately given the duties normally associated with a first or second year associate at a large firm. I was responsible for conducting discovery, writing chronologies from the documents, writing lines of questioning for, and second-chairing at depositions. Additionally, my engineering background allowed me to facilitate communication between our client (an engineering company) and the firm. My experiences at the firm have convinced me that I have the ability to work successfully a lawyer.

I firmly believe my experiences in law, engineering, civic activity, and political activism will allow me to be a creative and contributing member of the intellectual life at [school]. Thank you for your consideration.

Strengths

The author includes a lot of information regarding his background, his interests, and his experiences. One gets the impression that he will do well in law school.

Weaknesses

The essay could be more interesting and personal. Too many paragraphs are choppy and some are constructed of less than three sentences. The first three paragraphs could have easily been combined into one. The author should not have discussed the involvement of his brother and sister in on-campus activities because including the activities or achievements of anyone other than himself will not boost the quality of his own application.

ESSAY 4: Family/Ethnic Background; Native American; Environmental Activist

I met my great-grandmother through her diaries. I was ten years old. All my life "Grandma L" had just been a name I'd attached to a weathered face in yellow pictures, but as I read she came disturbingly to life. Hovering in the background of her prose are details which were a revelation to me then, and have resonated in my life ever since. The first of these was that my "pap" was not a blood-relation at all. My biological great-grandfather, Grandma L's first husband, was an alcoholic who was abusive when drunk. They were married but she left him; it took her three tries. When she finally escaped that small Arkansas farm, she cautioned her children never to speak their father's name in her presence. Out of respect or perhaps just habit they still don't, even now, so many years after her death. Which is why the next revelation was so startling. Near the end of the diary, in a passage describing how violently she ran away, Grandma L laments that in fleeing her husband she was robbed of her heritage as well.

Grandma L was [a Native American]; she passed for full-blood but probably wasn't. Her husband, T.J., was [a Native American] as well, though mixed. In 1920's Arkansas, where you were either "White" or "Colored," the union of two [Native Americans] was rare and becoming more so. Preserving bloodlines was something spoken of passionately in abstract, but in practice the hardships of such a union seemed futile if you could pass yourself and your family off as White. Facing the American Indian community in the small town near their farm after her failed attempts to leave seems to have permanently scarred Grandma L. Looked upon as a traitor to her race, she largely agreed with her detractors. So when she ran, she cut herself off from this guilt as well. She changed her hair, her manner of dress, basically everything except her name—determined that her children would never suffer for her "failings" and be mistaken for illegitimate. In this way, my family's heritage became a secret.

While the effect of this knowledge on my life has been substantial, it has also been gradual. I think my initial reaction was simply, "cool." I was ten, a hockey player, and very much drawn to my father's big Italian family. But it was a secret that [was] whispered to me often even then, and by high-school I was whispering back. My family moved south when I was in tenth grade and, as an advanced student, I was allowed to create an independent study course. While my efforts wound up at best a general survey of Southern American Indian history, the significance of what I'd learned over the course of two afternoons reading old diaries in an attic had begun to distill—as much as anything else, I was American Indian. But it was still something I wouldn't dare admit, even to my best friends.

Six months later I went to my first pow-wow and learned a most important lesson. As important, in retrospect, as any since that day in the attic. I had been shy about the experience, wandering and watching and a little embarrassed. Together with my parents we came upon a group

---

NOTE: Essay 4 is unusually long, and although it was successful, be advised that this circumstance is the exception and not the rule. It is much wiser to keep your submission to two pages or less.

of people learning a traditional dance of prayer. Out of the pack, a little blond girl with green eyes—not seven years old—approached with a smile and asked my mother, was she "native"? My mother didn't know what to say, and truly, neither did I until that very moment. "A little," I said. "Me too!" she replied and then asked us wouldn't we learn to dance with her? We did, and that was the last time I hid my heritage.

In college I pursued my heritage from a more academic bent. I joined "Native Americans at [school]" and participated in the campus community whenever possible. From these experiences were born the ideas which became the inspiration for the vast majority of my independent work Junior and Senior years. Mid-way through my junior year the first of these coalesced in my first Junior Paper. I'd gotten past debunking overtly racist history and moved on to something I believe is much more pervasive. Traditionally, American Indian history, oddly, has been about Whites and how, depending on your viewpoint, they either conquered, civilized, or raped what is now America. Indigenous peoples are subsumed by that story; they are passive, victimized, without agency in their own death saga. I was and continue to be convinced that American Indians were much more clever and pro-active than history is thus far willing to begrudge. This was the core of what eventually became a senior thesis that was awarded the [school] prize in American History, [school's] highest academic honor for independent work in History.

Following these ideas, I began to study William Cronon's *Changes in the Land*. I'd been studying the subtle and sustainable ways American Indians manipulated their environment to enhance its usefulness to them. I became fascinated by the intimate interaction of humanity and the environment, especially as described by Cronon. If you know how to read it, Cronon taught me, the history of America is written large upon the face of this continent. It seemed to me that Western cultures had forgotten their connections to the Earth and had not only chided, but punished indigenous people for remembering them. My curiosity for these connections was piqued, and I found myself drawn to indigenous rainforest peoples, for whom it seems a similar story unfolds even today. I joined Rainforest Conservancy as a member of the Education Group, and began to study these peoples in earnest. Together with many colleagues, I became heavily involved in a petition and lobbying effort aimed at the U.N. and O.A.S., the stated purpose of which was to impress upon these organizations the importance of indigenous peoples within rainforest environments. Rather than creating "preserves" free from human conduct, the indigenous rainforest peoples, and the rainforest itself, had to be understood within context. Development, not interaction, was the enemy of the rainforest, especially when these "preserves" were thinly disguised excuses for evicting indigenes from their traditional homelands, so that, five years hence when the world was no longer looking, the "preserves" would be opened to "limited" development with little fear of indigenous reprisal.

Our efforts were largely wasted, but I had been rudely introduced to the world of politics. Frustrated, I wanted to see the process from a different perspective and sought out an internship with my Congressman. Upon learning of my interest in American Indians, he asked me to seek out and attend any conference or hearing regarding Indian issues that I could, reporting back to him on any issue that might be of importance to his constituents. I did so happily over the course of that summer and the next. It wound up that the Congressman had a much stricter threshold than I when it came to what might interest the voters back home, but the experience was nonetheless fascinating. All throughout my studies I had read stories of an American government that was shameful in its treatment of American Indians. I was soon shocked by how little had changed. Whenever the Federal government extends a hand, it simultaneously turns its back as state governments use the offering as leverage to chip away at Indian autonomy—a pocketbook war on third-world nations hidden in plain sight of all America. Together with my frustrations concerning the environment, my anger at the state of American/Indian affairs is the source of my interest in the law.

American Indians and the environment need many things. Trite as it may sound, not the least of these is, frankly, the need for more than a few good lawyers. So I aim to become one. It is an odd, long road that has brought me to this point; a journey begun on another's feet upon what was little more than a dirt path leading away from a small Arkansas farm. I am excited to follow it further . . .

Strengths

This is a very interesting and well-written essay. It immediately grabs the attention of the reader. It has no awkward or forced transitions. It tells a story and demonstrates adequate experience and dedication to the author's ultimate goal, and how law school will help her achieve it.

Weaknesses

It is a bit too long. The ending is unfortunately the weak point. The author's reason for wanting to attend law school is quickly thrown into the conclusion, which does come off, despite the author's efforts to the contrary, as a bit "trite."

ESSAY 5: Student Journalist; Big Brother

During my three years at [school], my involvement in activities ranging from community service to journalism has been characterized by a desire to better understand the social utility of a single characteristic that links them all: communication. Communication is an incredibly broad term, but through my extracurricular experiences, I have unraveled some of its complexity and developed a personal vision for its use.

Journalism is perhaps the most obvious forum in which I have attempted to both understand and positively affect the role of communication in my community. The [name], the only daily news source on [school's] campus, serves the role of both informing the college community and generating lively debate within that community. I joined the staff during my freshman year as a news writer with the intent of contributing to the informative side of the paper. But during that year, I grew dissatisfied with the level of debate that took place on the campus. The editorial pages and campus discourse in general were dominated by the same recycled arguments regarding the Greek system and the College's alcohol policy, while other equally important topics such as gender, race and [school's] changing curriculum went largely unnoticed. Ultimately, I felt confined in my role as a messenger of information; I wanted to comment on that information.

Thus, during my sophomore year, I made the transition to the editorial side of the newspaper. A year later I became the Editorials Editor, a position that gave me an unparalleled opportunity to promote lively, meaningful debate among thousands of people each day. I perceived myself as less of a journalist in the professional sense and more of an objective moderator and facilitator of an ongoing, community-wide debate. On a campus that is not known for having a particularly vocal student body, this task was especially challenging. Indeed, apathy inhibited open communication, which, in turn, allowed stereotypes and misunderstanding to persist. So, I actively sought out opinions on news-making issues. I held weekly meetings with my staff to discuss ideas worthy of debate. I worked with writers to turn events into issues. I employed all of these strategies with the idea that greater dialogue between columnists would spill onto the editorial pages and then into dorm rooms, lounges and cafeterias.

As a responsible journalist, however, I realized the importance of communication being fair and accurate, especially in controversial columns. In one instance, a female student submitted an editorial detailing how an administrator allegedly mishandled her claim of sexual harassment by a student leader. I recognized that the column raised issues that were of great importance to the campus—sexual assault and the administration's way of dealing with it—while at the same time, I knew that a false statement could potentially ruin the argument as well as the administrator's reputation. My pairing of responsibility with a recognition of the value of communication guided me in my editing of the column, which, when published, resulted in the formation of two student groups that examined sexual assault on [school's] campus. This experience taught me the power that a reasoned argument has in effecting change in society.

Through my participation in [school's] Big Brother/Big Sister Program, I have found that discourse is not confined to the mass media, nor should it be. Indeed, for me, community service has been an exercise in communication. At the most fundamental level, dialogue must take place between individuals. As a Big Brother, I have seen how discourse between two individuals can bridge the chasms of generational, geographic and socioeconomic differences. I take great pride in knowing that I have exposed, my Little Brother, who lives in a poorly insulated assemblage of plywood, glass, and sheet metal, to Tuscan history, the benefits of higher education, and a place called Kentucky. And just as he has grown from this interaction, I have gained a greater understanding of a segment of the population that I could have overlooked, as many students do, during my four years at [school]. Indeed, our relationship has taught me the important quality of compassion.

The end of these experiences, for me, has not been just a better understanding of the role of communication in our society. Rather, they have impelled me to become an active player in this discourse. Half a century ago, Zechariah Chafee wrote, "We must do more than remove the discouragements to open discussion. We must exert ourselves to supply active encouragement." These words, and the experiences I described above, have inspired me to follow this urging.

Strengths

The essay is fairly interesting and portrays an image of the author as a very motivated individual who takes an active role in issues that matter to her. The theme of communication was a good forum for her to present her activism and sense of justice through her actions, not her words. As an effective communicator, she is also providing evidence that she could become a successful attorney.

Weaknesses

The author has several sentences that are too long. The reasons for wanting to attend law school and the way in which the degree will enhance the author's career could be more clearly defined.

ESSAY 6: Experience in Kenya

I was released from the Lamu hospital on a Monday morning. I still felt terrible, but I did not vocalize my thoughts. After spending three days in the open-air facility suffering through a case of amoebic dysentery, I looked forward to returning to the house where I was staying with other students.

The family of cats that roamed the corridors of the hospital had started to become more aggressive, and the sole modern toilet had broken two days earlier. I smiled at the nurse with whom I had fought about needles, thanked the doctor who had misdiagnosed me with malaria, and hobbled to the waiting dhow. I hoped to attend my Kiswahili lesson that afternoon.

To my chagrin, I could not attend my lesson, nor could I attend the following day. In the days following my release from the hospital, my body seemed to be falling apart. After only two weeks in Kenya, I was too sick to move. I fainted when I stood up and felt dizzy when I lay down. Hearing about my condition, my Swahili tutor, a young woman from Lamu, came to visit me with a donkey cart in tow. I realized she wanted to take my to another doctor. I felt too drained to protest, and so I went.

Fatma is the women's health practicioner of Lamu. I recognized her when my tutor and I arrived at her house, as she had given a lecture to my group on "Women and Islam." She motioned for me to lie down on the floor, asked about my pain, and ran her hands across my forehead and stomach. She said nothing. She seemed to understand my symptoms, and I hoped she would quickly prescribe some medicine so I could go home and sleep.

Instead, Fatma placed a lit candle on my bare stomach. Over the candle, she suctioned a small glass jar to my flesh and scattered some herbs around the jar. While rubbing my abdomen, she began to chant softly under her breath with her eyes closed. After a series of chants, she would gasp for breath, pause, and begin to chant again. After a few minutes I noticed that tears were streaming down Fatma's face as she chanted.

The ritual continued for a few more minutes, and then she stopped. She leaned over my face and said fiercely, "Have you been eating in public places?" I nodded, expecting to hear the lecture on sanitation and drinking water which I had received at the hospital. "You have been cursed."

She explained that someone who was hungry had watched me eat, and had put a curse on me to punish me for not sharing. "Make sure you share what you have," she warned me. "If you do, you will be healthy. If you do not, your life will be filled with curses." With those words, she left me with a bill for twenty dollars, some salty greens to chew on twice a day, and a prescription for life.

Strengths

This is a unique and interesting personal statement. It will certainly stand out from the stacks of essays with which it will be read. The applicant has taken a risk by not mentioning her motivation to attend law school nor any of her achievements. Instead she hopes that her gift for storytelling and the impact that this experience had on her will impress upon the admissions committee that she is a worldly candidate whose experience in a third-world country left her with a new outlook on life—a "prescription" to help others. Her risk obviously paid off.

Weaknesses

This is not the sort of risk that an applicant without outstanding credentials should take. If you are unsure of your chances of getting into law school, you need to use the essay as your chance to show off your relevant experience, your achievements, and your capacity to excel. Your motivations to attend law school should also be addressed. This essay also has a couple of obvious typos.

ESSAY 7: Management and Chemistry Major; Stock Market Experience; College Pro Painter

Many people criticize required college courses and what others study as being useless in the real world. They do not see any practical skills being developed, so they automatically label it as unproductive, but what they miss is the personal development of every student, which is more important than the acquisition of skills. Everyone, either consciously or not, uses their four years at school to find where they belong in the world. My undergraduate years have been a continuing exploration of myself, wherein I have constantly learned more and more about who I want to be.

High school never required that I determine what I wanted to study. I knew that there were a few areas that I enjoyed more than others, but other than that I never gave it much thought. I was always more proficient in science and mathematics than anything else, but I decided to enter the school of management at [school]. I chose management out of admiration of my father, who immigrated to this country from Italy at age eight, was the only child out of eleven to graduate from college, and then went on to become a successful entrepreneur in the restaurant and real estate businesses.

During the first weeks of my freshman year, I was presented with a unique opportunity. I could graduate in three years or study an entire other major, due to advanced placement credits from high school. After weighing the benefits of either choice, I decided that I wanted to study chemistry, a subject I had always favored in high school. Although a years worth of tuition was tempting, I knew that four years would be best for me as a growth process, as well as satisfy a latent desire to study a science. My finance and chemistry studies have enhanced my analytical abilities and helped me to develop a methodical and intuitive thinking process. The exposure to two very different disciplines has been extremely rewarding.

My employment during my undergraduate years has been very educational as well. Working for Schering-Plough and Mabon Securities gave me a detailed introduction to the stock market from two opposing sides. At Schering we talked about our stock to people I later worked for at Mabon, however, my employment as a College Pro franchisee was an incredible experience and valuable lesson in the dealings of small business management and customer relations. College Pro franchises a name, gives some basic training in house painting, logistic support, and then sends franchisees out on their own to acquire equipment, hire workers, book jobs, and do everything else required to run a small business. I was required to attend to every detail, no matter how minute, in order to maintain a smooth operation, between customers, workers, and retailers, I dealt with at least twenty people a week, all of whom relied on me to provide something for them. Running a small business required a level of attention that I had never had to maintain before, but I found that I was capable of keeping everything under control.

My decision to attend law school is an outgrowth of my development as a student and a desire to enter an analytical and prestigious field. My undergraduate studies and work experience have prepared me well for the study of the law, both have taught me the discipline required, as well as engendered the academic ability necessary to excel. I may never use my knowledge in chemistry or finance for professional reasons, but my studies have not been impractical. My undergraduate education transcends practicality, it is an integral part of myself that affects everything I do in life.

Strengths

This is a straightforward and standard personal statement for an applicant applying immediately after college. In a soundly structured essay, the applicant discusses his undergraduate experience, his jobs to date, and his motivations for attending law school.

Weaknesses

The essay is not very compelling and does not explain well enough the motivation for attending law school. Since the applicant does not have much practical experience, he could have used the opportunity to branch out and tell a personal story that would reveal more about his personality and make him more likeable and memorable to the committee. The essay obviously did not hurt his chances of getting into law school, but had other areas of his application not been strong, it probably wouldn't have done much to help him stand out.

ESSAY 8: Peace Corps in Honduras; Analyst of Latin America Labor Conditions

After college I served for two and a half years in Honduras with the U.S. Peace Corps. During my time there I worked on several development projects. My experiences left me with mixed feelings about development and what is realistically achievable. Projects often proved only thin band-aids against larger endemic problems. I found potential for changing some of the larger problems of development in a surprising arena, *maquiladoras*, or textile factories.

While in Honduras, I talked to many women who worked in *maquiladoras*. Unlike what I had read in classes, these women were happy to have their jobs and suffered no health problems or abuse. They earned more money working in the factories in the cities than picking coffee in the mountains. Women could leave their homes and find work without having to depend on husbands or families to survive.

The factory jobs had other positive side effects. I saw wealthy families driving to the countryside to find maids because all the city maids quit to work in the factories where they earned more. Wages for domestic workers had already risen and these families were trying to avoid paying an even higher salary. Also, factories required a sixth grade degree. This, if nothing else, could motivate an illiterate farmer to keep his daughters in school.

How to balance these positive factors with the often exploitative and abusive methods of the factory managers, or how to control the problems of rural-urban migration are questions I am still investigating. However, economic opportunities outside of the home, such as those in *maquiladoras*, could play a key role in changing traditional attitudes that prevent women from developing and using their full potential.

With the new U.S. policy focus on trade with Latin America and with more and more businesses using labor abroad, labor conditions in *maquiladoras* will be a growing human rights issue. At the Washington

Office on Latin America (WOLA), I have been able to write letters to the USTR pushing for the continued review of the Generalized System of Preferences in Guatemala, to the President of El Salvador to encourage the enforcement of their labor codes, and lobbied for a labor petitioning amendment to the Caribbean Basin Trade Security Act.

A law degree would give me a tool to continue to work effectively and realistically on this and other issues that contribute to the well-being of people affected by U.S. policies and investments in Latin America.

Strengths

The essay is short but effective. It has one central theme, which is tied into the brief conclusion and to the author's motivation for attending law school. It says nothing of the author's college experience, but since this can be found elsewhere on the application, it is a smart omission.

Weaknesses

The conclusion could be strengthened by expanding the paragraph to more than one sentence and by being more specific about how the law degree will be used.

ESSAY 9: Career in International Environmental Protection; Political Lobbyist

In early June, I sat in a Capitol Hill office with congressional staff and my fellow advocates watching as the Congress passed the bill implementing an international environmental agreement. As the votes were counted, we cheered and congratulated ourselves—our list of accomplishments appeared long. The bill would create a [multi-lateral environmental protection program and a Secretariat]. The Congressional vote was, for me, a personal and professional triumph, representing a milestone in my seven-year career focused on protection of the international environment.

My decision to apply to [school] Law School arises from my experience with [the international environmental agreement]. From the earliest negotiations through to my current job at the [Secretariat of the international environmental agreement], I have participated in environmental policy making on a number of levels and from a variety of perspectives. Each step has given me a better understanding of the roles of governments, international institutions, and individuals in environmental protection.

However, I have also come to realize that a thorough knowledge of law and legal frameworks is critical to my career goals. A law degree will build upon my professional experience by providing me with the skills I need to effectively approach the complexities of international environmental problems. At the same time, I bring to law school, and a legal career, considerable knowledge of environmental issues, significant work as an advocate, and experience in international negotiations and policy making.

As a policy analyst and advocate with [an environmental NGO] I cooperated closely with public-interest groups from [around the world] as we developed and negotiated the [international agreement]. My experience living in [Latin American country] and Spanish fluency allowed me to work closely with [Latin American advocates], and often put me in the position of mediator when American and [Latin American] environmentalists disagreed. In the end, the strong coalition among environmentalists from [developing and developed countries] was critical to developing proposals that were acceptable to all governments. In the process I not only acquired significant mediation and consensus building experience, but also participated in developing unique policy solutions that were acceptable to all national governments.

The [international agreement] negotiations were a clear lesson to me that good advocacy is more than just eloquent argument. Researching the details of a subject, knowing the laws and rules, and understanding opposing positions are also critical tools of good negotiation and advocacy.

When environmentalists first sat down with government lawyers, we seemed to lose every round because we were not familiar with the all relevant legal and political frameworks. Developing workable policy proposals required a knowledge of the [many international agreements and domestic laws and policy objectives]. Involvement in this policy making challenge provided me with excellent training in strategic negotiation and effective advocacy techniques, in addition to giving me significant motivation for acquiring a legal education.

My work after the agreement was signed taught me the importance of follow-through in successful policy advocacy. I lobbied Congress in support of the agreement, and after the vote I worked on implementation. As with most international agreements, and domestic laws, much was left open to interpretation. I spent months discussing confidentiality rules, public access procedures, funding levels and staffing with government policy makers from signatory countries. To ensure that [developing country] environmentalists were included in the process, I initiated, organized and led a workshop to draft recommendations to governments. Though we were successful in preserving much our original intent, failure is also an excellent teacher. As I watched what I thought were groundbreaking public participation clauses dissolve into nothing,

I received an unforgettable lesson about the difference between "shall," "should" and "may."

Managing a project designing international approaches to [environmental problems] for the [secretariat of the international environmental agreement] I have obtained an inside perspective on governmental institutions and their limits and potential. I am also in the privileged, and sometimes humbling position of working for an institution I fought to create.

The perspective shift from advocate to government is valuable. For example, I have gained sympathy for maligned bureaucrats as I explained repeatedly to my ex-colleagues in the environmental community why the [Secretariat] can not follow their recommendations. At the same time, I realize that I truly enjoy the role of advocate—a bit of introspection that influenced my decision to pursue a career as an attorney.

By taking on [complex international environmental policy], I have had the opportunity to apply many of the lessons I learned from the [international agreement negotiation] to another international environmental problem. As I try to juggle the objectives of governments, industry and public interest groups, my experience in building diverse coalitions, lobbying for support, and negotiating deals is valuable. And perhaps more than any other phase of my career, the complexity of creating fair, equitable and economically viable international systems to [improve environment protection] has made me realize that I will need legal training if I plan to continue this type of work.

At [environmental NGO] and the [international agreement secretariat] I have developed an understanding of environmental issues and the increasingly international nature of environmental policy. Given my background and my future career plans, the strong environmental curriculum and faculty of [school] made it an obvious law school choice. [School's] excellent reputation in environment and natural resources law, and opportunities for interdisciplinary cooperation were important factors in my decision to apply. Finally, I am convinced that an important element of law school is learning from other students. [School's] student body has the reputation for excellence and diversity of experience that is important to me.

Strengths

The applicant backs up his passion for environmental protection by an in-depth description of his related work. He has also researched the particular school for which the essay was written and explains why it is the school that he wants to attend. He comes across as focused and ready to move on to the next phase in his career.

ESSAY 10: University Scholar; Strong Academics; Community Service

As a graduating senior at [school], I was asked to serve on the Selection Committee for the University Scholars Program. Eager to give back to a program which has afforded me so many opportunities, I accepted the invitation without hesitation. Like so many other opportunities presented to me at [school], I could not have imagined just how challenging and fulfilling this experience would be. As I sat at the conference table, trying to absorb both the insight and expectations of the senior members of the Selection Committee (many of whom had interviewed me just four years earlier), I could not help but reflect upon my own role as a University Scholar.

A scholarship based on both academic performance and community service/leadership, it was clear to me from the beginning that the University wished for Scholars to continue such worthwhile endeavors as [school] students. I decided then, as I continue to believe now, that the best way to demonstrate my appreciation for the generosity and confidence shown in me, by the University and the its Associates, was to not only uphold, but to surpass the standards set by the University Scholars Program.

So started my four-year endeavor at [school]. Yes, my two-fold plan for success was a careful design. My objectives were simple: (1) to preserve my role as a Scholar by integrating myself into the University community as both a student and a leader, and (2) to do all in my power to prepare myself for the well-known "rigors" of law school.

Ironically, the fulfillment of my four-year, two-fold plan would begin earlier than I ever expected. I had not even graduated from [High School] when I attended my first University Scholar's meeting. All I remember was that I briefly introduced myself, offered one or two suggestions, and departed the Community Services Coordinator. While I am not completely certain how my new position came about, I do know that my involvement simply continued from that day forward. In fact, in promising to make the most of my four years at [school], I made it a point to take advantage of every opportunity available to increase the diversity, as well as, the quality of my involvement on campus.

To my own benefit, I realize now that I extended that promise to all areas of my life. The determination with which I tackled University activities allowed me to maintain my role as a campus leader, without foregoing professional job opportunities and local community involvement. Admittedly, my schedule was a bit overwhelming at times. However,

I cannot begin to explain the life lessons to be learn through such endeavors. The diversity of people, situations, and events has, in my opinion, strengthened both my character and my intellect.

However, without question, no area demonstrates more clearly my commitment to my four-year, two-fold plan than my academic performance at [school]. Traumatized by experts who predicted G.P.A. declines for college freshman and anxious about the University Scholars' G.P.A. requirement, I realized very early in my collegiate career that my most significant achievement would have to be in the classroom. Reminding myself constantly of President Lincoln's words, *"Always bear in mind that your own resolution to succeed is more important than any one other thing."*, I set about the task at hand. Not attempting to learn the law as an undergraduate, I selected courses which exposed me to the dynamics of our legal system, and more importantly, challenged and prepared me for the study of law. For example, I chose philosophy courses to sharpen my reasoning skills, writing courses to provide for greater competence and style, and minored in speech communication in order to master the art of verbal expression and debate. After tackling and conquering such a demanding course of study, I am more confident than ever of my ability to handle the intensity of law school.

I have not yet met an individual whose life did not involve circumstances. Therefore, I have come to believe that judgment should not lie in the quantity of struggle, but rather in the quality of the character that results. I have, to this point in my life, done all that I can to prepare myself for this endeavor. As I have worked since I was fourteen years old, I am a true believer in hard work and opportunities earned. I desire the opportunity to share my knowledge and insight, to continue my education in preparation for my professional career, and most importantly, to one day contribute to a legal system with which I am so taken. Your consideration of my application is in all reality a review of my efforts to fulfill my four-year, two-fold plan. I hope you find, as I believe, that I come well-prepared.

Strengths

This applicant's strengths were her GPA and her LSAT. Her essay obviously did not keep her out of law school, but it was not an asset to her application.

Weaknesses

The essay is poorly written and includes obvious typos and grammatical errors. It does not explain with any evidence the candidate's motivation to attend law school nor why she might be qualified to do so. She speaks of very little that can't be found elsewhere in her application.

ESSAY 11: English Doctoral Candidate; Volunteer at the ACLU; Issue Analyst of Prisoners' Rights

When I began volunteering at the American Civil Liberties Union of Michigan, I was a doctoral candidate in English literature, a budding scholar of the early novel. By the time I stopped volunteering ten months later, I had learned that I wanted to become a litigator, a lawyer who brought his political beliefs and persuasive writing to bear on some of the most important social issues of the day. My experiences at the A.C.L.U. opened my eyes not only to the complexity and urgency of impassioned legal work but also to my own professional aspirations.

Under the supervision of the A.C.L.U.'s generous and busy legal director, I was quickly exposed to many aspects of practical lawyering. My first job—assessing and responding to the organization's voluminous mail—required me to analyze the fact patterns that various correspondents presented. The many incoming accounts of police brutality, judicial indifference, and prison rape were often moving and frequently suspect. They forced me to temper my emotional responses and determine whether the complaints seemed both factually plausible and within the A.C.L.U.'s limited purview. After this challenging introduction, I was then asked to assist in the discovery phase of a prisoner's rights case. This work was detailed and intricate: my job was to reconstruct the specific events of a day from long ago from years, while searching for conflicts between the prison's official regulations and the actual conduct of its guards. As I called Michigan prisons for information, sifted through ten years of our client's prison records, and helped endlessly revise our pleadings, I learned a good deal about the small chores and thankless legal persistence that go into building cases.

At the same time, I found considerable overlap between my new legal tasks and my ongoing academic work. In an A.C.L.U. case I assisted in, for example, a judge overturned a state ban on partial birth abortion because the procedure had no precise meaning in the medical lexicon, and the legislation might thus chill a wide variety of medical practices. What fascinated me was that when confronted with the task of interpreting a knotty and important text, the twentieth-century legal system made many of the same interpretive moves as the eighteenth-century novel readers I had studied in my English graduate work. As the case unfolded, the pleadings debated the legislators' authorial intentions; the relevant Supreme Court and Sixth Circuit precedents; the contradictory testimony of various medical experts; and, finally, the language of the statute itself. Like my eighteenth-century readers, modern textual interpreters were attempting to make sense of a silent, ambiguous document by finding ways to situate it within different historical, intertextual, and linguistic contexts. While particular interpretive conventions have changed over the centuries—modern lawyers cite prior cases and not

Biblical parables to bolster their arguments—I came to realize that the broader task of comprehending texts (whether artistic expression or legislation) has not. Moreover, as I roamed through the stacks of Michigan's graduate and law libraries, I increasingly began to believe that it is precisely through interpretation, *through* embracing particular readings of *Robinson Crusoe* over others or through fighting over the legal standing of terms such as "partial birth abortion" that a society obliquely expresses its priorities and values as well as its blind spots.

I began making these connections partly because my work on the prisoner's rights case had forced me to question my own values and unspoken assumptions. Was I being co-opted by working on behalf of an unrepentant racist and murderer who complained at having some writings and a swastika confiscated by prison officials? Or was I defending the rights of future prisoners who might be writing less like our client and more like John Bunyan, Henry David Thoreau, or Martin Luther King, Jr.? Had I succumbed to the knee-jerk First Amendment absolutism that the A.C.L.U. is sometimes accused of? I thought I knew what public policy I supported but I became sorely aware of my legal ignorance: much as I needed to do so, I felt ill-equipped to objectively assess and synthesize the various judicial precedents that pertained to the case. Although I was frustrated by my uncertainties and limited knowledge, I found myself increasingly excited by the questions I was trying to ask. By the time I finally threw myself into the bittersweet task of assisting a murderer, I had learned both how little I knew of the law and how much I valued the nuanced, committed defense of civil liberties.

My volunteer work left me wanting to do more in the legal sphere. While the law may be too ungainly and inefficient a vehicle to directly change the world, it offers a unique opportunity to help influence people's interpretation of their world. With the knowledge and skills imparted by a legal education, I hope to get back to crafting public arguments over abortion, prisoners' rights, Internet expression, and other defining issues of our day.

Strengths

This is a very well-written essay. Its main topic, a volunteer experience, showcases some experience in the field, but more importantly, the author's critical thinking skills and his motivations for further study are evidenced. He comes across as an interesting person who would likely do well in law school.

Weaknesses

None.

ESSAY 12: Activist for Gay Rights and Reproductive Health Issues; Feminist; Democratic Campaign Experience

I am an activist with a commitment to fighting for progressive causes through legislation, policy, and grassroots organizing. While I have participated in many varied projects from editing a sexuality education curriculum to campaigning for gay rights as a local boardmember of [the statewide gay rights organization], I am most concerned with reproductive health issues. In this statement I will explain how I gained expertise in this field through both academic and professional work. Through this work I have acquired the intellectual foundation and the concrete experience to be an effective advocate for citizens' right to sexuality education and health care.

At [school] I began my commitment to reproductive health. I earned the right to design my own major in women's studies and legal issues, for which I took courses in feminism and wrote on the developing legal precedent recognizing fetal rights. During my year at [school] I studied the impact the abortion pill RU 486 might have on the National Health Service, researched the evolving debate about the drug in the European press, and presented my findings at a Women's Studies Department seminar upon my return to the U.S. In my senior thesis on the legal treatment of pregnant substance abusers, I addressed the difficulties associated with prosecuting these women and proposed alternative approaches.

While I was a student, I gained professional experience as a birth control counselor at the University health clinic. I also worked as a Planned Parenthood educator, for which I edited a sexuality education curriculum and designed and taught community programs on contraception, AIDS, puberty, and sexual abuse prevention.

When I moved to a small desert town in the Western United States, I volunteered for a democratic congressional campaign, where I briefed the candidate on abortion rights and sexuality issues in health care reform. I met the executive director of the regional Planned Parenthood, and convinced her to hire me as the agency's first Director of Public Affairs. I coordinated grassroots lobbying efforts on pending legislation including the state's health care reform bill, clinic access bill, and anti-gay rights legislation.

I quickly learned that this small town was far more conservative than my university's eastern college community. Many of Planned Parenthood's efforts to promote sexuality education were thwarted. I decided to discover who opposed the agency and what their tactics were. My research uncovered a network of local activists, some of whom had connections to state and nationwide Conservative organizations. I attended many meetings and followed public right-wing activity such as the campaign to teach creationism in our local schools. I published my findings in an op-ed piece for our local paper, and as a front page article for a west-coast human rights newsletter. I have enclosed copies of these publications for you.

When my State Senator asked me to manage his reelection campaign, I eagerly accepted since I knew he had worked hard in support of health care and civil rights. The position also offered me greater professional responsibility. Even though we lost the election, the campaign was an invaluable lesson in creating an effective political message, managing hundreds of volunteers, working in coalition with other campaigns, designing advertising, and fundraising.

I had hoped to work in the state capitol after the campaign, and I am now working for a state level health care advocacy organization which employs a lobbyist and coordinates grassroots strategy. In my new position I am researching legislation, helping the director design lobbying strategies, and keeping affiliated organizations throughout the state informed about evolving policy and bills.

While I believe that I have developed both academic and professional expertise in reproductive health policy, health care reform, and political organizing, I would like to acquire the skills and power to make a bigger difference. Law school would provide me with the technical skills and professional influence to be more effective in confronting right-wing litigation and initiatives and in designing and advocating for progressive social policy. After law school, I envision working for a non-profit organization such as the ACLU Reproductive Freedom Project, or working in government drafting and analyzing reproductive health policy and legislation.

Strengths

This essay is well written and structured. By unveiling her work experience, and the controversial issues that they revolved around, much can also be inferred about the applicant's personality. Her motivation to attend law school and the way that a law degree will enhance her career are unquestioned because of the experiences that she shares in the essay.

Weaknesses

None.

ESSAY 13: Family Background; Mexican-American; Corporate Law Experience; Criminal Law Intern; Volunteer Paralegal

I come from a family that believes in education. We believe that education gives freedom; the freedom to choose one's future, the freedom to help others, and the freedom to accept and appreciate different ways of thinking. I have been nurtured in an environment that taught me that I could achieve anything as long as I was prepared. "You will succeed" is a phrase so often heard in my home, that self-confidence and determination are qualities very much a part of us all. I am a first generation Mexican-American whose parents were the first in their families to get higher educations. They have taught my brothers and me to exercise our capabilities to the fullest; to fulfill our potentials through experiences inside and outside the doors of academia.

The desire to study law is driven by the need to contribute to society; I must make a positive impact. This education will foster my most important goals—the ability to help those in need, a lifetime of learning, and the opportunity to work in diverse fields. I am determined to become an attorney. It is a profession where my creative thinking, analytical writing skills and sense of civic duty will be most valuable and useful. Professionally and personally, I will be fulfilled.

My entry into the world of law came soon after graduation. Working as a bankruptcy paralegal in a Wall Street firm, I was immediately immersed in the corporate and litigation arenas. Being familiar with the workings of large institutions through internships at CBS Evening News and the State Department, I adapted well to the demanding environment where the ability to learn quickly and to perform efficiently were necessities. I was managing seven large corporate bankruptcy cases, drafting and researching pleadings, and preparing and filing multi-million dollar fee applications within a month.

Although my experience in corporate law was valuable, I soon became interested in working with clients on a more personal level. Fortunately, I was offered a summer internship in the criminal law department of a medium-sized firm in Mexico. This opportunity allowed me not only to learn about a different country's legal system, but also enabled me to see the significant differences between American corporate law and the Mexican criminal justice system. Working in Mexico permitted close interaction with clients in jail and prison settings. Being able to assist these persons through research and legal support in court revealed the possibilities of what a criminal justice system could offer. I began to more fully understand the power a law degree could have to help individuals as well as large institutions.

By the end of the internship, I knew I wanted more exposure working with people. I soon became a volunteer paralegal with a non-profit legal organization for the lower-income population of Buffalo. Interviewing and educating clients in shelters and soup kitchens has been one of the most personally satisfying jobs I have had. I have learned about the legal intricacies of public assistance programs while working with Latinos and other people of color in the U.S.—a population that is extremely important to me. Having the capability to offer a service to a community that has given me so much has been an invaluable experience.

In the time that I have had to explore some of the dimensions of law, I have seen the tremendous impact that attorneys can have. It is a profession that, above all, allows people to help others. I am ready for the responsibilities of law school. I have the capability, the perspective, and the commitment to become a lawyer; I am prepared to take on the social and civic duties that this vocation demands.

Strengths

The essay has a strong introduction. It is for the most part, well written and structured. Interesting and relevant experiences are relayed and motivations for attending law school are addressed.

Weaknesses

The theme of wanting to help people is stated but not backed up well enough. It is unclear exactly what the applicant will do with the law degree.

ESSAY 14: Family Background; Art History Major; Nonprofit Paralegal Experience

I was raised in the San Joaquin Valley, an agricultural region in California between the Coast Range and the Sierra Nevada. Although my parents were not farmers, they lived on a farm, and from the time I was nine I spent several hours a day helping the field workers and doing odd jobs after school—mowing lawns, delivering papers and, when I got older, running a small home-cleaning service. My family depended on me to help to make ends meet, so I could not take time off if problems came up; I had to make do.

My responsibilities to the household denied me some of the usual pleasures of childhood, but they made me tougher and left me with a practical turn of mind that has served me well. By the time I graduated from high school, I had decided that a career in public service would allow me to apply my pragmatism to problems of social consequence, and that a legal education would best equip me to resolve these problems.

I chose to attend [school] because it has a good school of public policy. But a required course on cultural interpretation that I took in my freshman year persuaded me that a broader undergraduate education would be more interesting and might ultimately serve me better. So I changed my plans and concentrated in art history and took elective courses in philosophy and political theory. Although these subjects have little obvious application to the career I hope to pursue, studying them has allowed me to think about the values different societies have chosen to uphold or dismiss. As an attorney I will need to think along similar lines when I assess legislation written to maintain or change these values.

My current work as a paralegal at a non-profit law office has taught me much about law's social import. While I have observed how clumsy legal rights can be in their attempt to satisfy individual needs with general entitlements, I have also seen the symbolic importance these rights hold for the neediest and how effective their judicious defense can be. And while I have learned how difficult it is for litigators alone to alter the existing order fundamentally, I have also seen the great potential of a grassroots agency to cultivate rulings that bring about modest but valuable change. This work is needed, and I want to do it.

Strengths

The first two paragraphs of the essay are personal and interesting. They grab the reader's attention and set the stage for a pleasing essay.

Weaknesses

Unfortunately, the final two paragraphs do not follow the nice setup that the opening provided. The essay has grammatical errors. While reasons are offered for wanting to attend law school, they should be supported by the experiences relayed. The applicant's post-law school plans are too vague.

ESSAY 15: Career Switcher; Teacher of Talmudic Law

Having spent the last ten years studying and teaching Talmudic Law, I have often been asked to describe what I study and teach. What is Talmudic Law?

By way of answer here is an example. In the beginning of Tractate Yebamoth the Talmud discusses the following case. Reuben's granddaughter marries Simon, Reuben's brother and Simon later takes a second wife. Normally if Simon were to die without having had children, according to the law of levirate marriage which states that the wife of a man who dies childless must marry her deceased husband's brother, one of Simon's wives would have to marry Reuben. In this case, however because one of Simon's wives is Reuben's granddaughter, neither Reuben's granddaughter nor Simon's second wife would need to marry Reuben. The Talmud, however, describes an exception to the preceding rule. If Reuben's granddaughter is biologically unable to have children, then Simon's second wife would have to marry Reuben. The reasoning for this exception is complicated, and not necessary to illustrate my point. Almost the entire tractate of Yebamoth which is one hundred and twenty-two folio pages in length, addresses similar cases. Although there are numerous issues addressed in the Talmud which are more practical than the previous example, there are many others that are even more implausible. Indeed parts of the Talmud make the age-old question about angels on the head of a pin seem practical.

When I describe the Talmud to people and tell them how long I have spent studying it and describe the energy required to properly analyze the issues involved in the various cases, they almost always ask me why I find it so interesting. Why does analyzing these purely hypothetical cases hold any interest to me?

The answer, I feel, is that if one simply looks to the Talmud for laws concerning day-to-day life then, yes, one will be disappointed since the Talmud does seem to waste much time on cases that exist only in theory. I, however, have looked to the Talmud for the beauty of its logic and have therefore found it fascinating. The Talmud has its own logical rules which govern its more than thirty tractates. The work of the student of the Talmud is to use these rules to help resolve the many questions that invariably arise. Typical questions that need to be addressed include: 1) What is the basis for the law? 2) What is the reasoning behind the law? 3) Would the law be the same even if the facts of the case were slightly different? and 4) Whether the principle stated in the case being studied is in agreement with a principle stated in another part of the Talmud? Answering one question usually creates another, thus leading one on a captivating search for understanding. Working with this interplay of logic has been one of the most enjoyable things I have ever done.

When I began teaching Talmudic law I found another opportunity to enjoy its logic. When lecturing on Talmudic law one must explain and clarify extremely complicated points of reasoning. Also many lectures must be put into writing. It is quite difficult to distill a lengthy and complex disagreement into two concise positions. However, the satisfaction I received when passages that had been obscure suddenly became completely clear, made it well worth the effort.

In conclusion, the forgoing raises an obvious question. If I enjoyed Talmudic law so much why am I looking for a career in law? The answer, quite simply, is that in choosing a career I have looked for an opportunity to utilize the analytic and communication skills that I have developed and enjoyed in the study and teaching of Talmudic law. In addition as I have grown older I have realized that I would like to be able to see the practical benefits of my work in addition to the intellectual enjoyment. The study and practice of law would be just such an opportunity.

Strengths

The applicant demonstrates how his interest in Talmudic law has led him on a logical path toward law school. The theme is probably one of a kind, so it will likely stand out.

Weaknesses

It has grammatical errors, which make it more difficult to read. The level of detail in which the Talmudic laws are discussed could have hurt the candidate because they aren't easy to follow. The essay may have been more compelling if less detail had been paid to the laws themselves and a more general discussion followed about how the applicant's career might progress after law school.

ESSAY 16: Korean Woman; Business Background; Interest in International Trade Law

To study law in American law school is the intersection of three sets composing my life: my belief in international trade, my interest in establishing international trade law based on economic principles, and the contribution that I can make as a Korean woman.

I believe that economy is the basis of society. People act according to their economic interest no matter what they are taught at school or at church. Economic power is the fundamental power which decides political power and cultural development. When a possibility of mutual gain exists, two countries develop and maintain a relationship. We see business entrepreneurs take initiative in building economic relationship before amity between two countries is accomplished. On the other hand, economic conflicts between two parties result in trouble and sometimes war. Virtually every war breaks out because of economic conflicts. Sometimes a war is disguised as a fight for freedom of religion, sometimes as a battle for restoring the dignity of a nation, but the true reason is almost always material gain.

In the globalized modern world, among many economic activities, international trade is the most important. International trade not only increases the wealth of all the parties involved but also promote cultural exchange. With all these advantages, international trade should be fostered. However, conflicts cannot be avoided. Preventing them by making faultless contracts and resolving problems when they appear can help reduce the possible causes of war and therefore contribute to world peace as well as increasing wealth. Preventing and resolving the conflicts are the two things that I would like to do as an international lawyer. There is one more thing I would like to do.

In high school I was taught, particularly in national ethics class, that I should sacrifice myself for my family, community, and country. If everybody pursues his/her individual interest only, our society will turn into chaos, with violence everywhere and every day, the strong controlling the week. It could be true that unselfishness plays an important part in social stability in some cases. However, a system that lets people naturally pursue their own interest and at the same time assures social order is more efficient and easier to enforce than an unnatural one which forces people to give up opportunity unwillingly.

Business administration and economics, my major and minor subject at university, showed me it was possible to set up such a system. Economics, first of all, assumes that every individual maximizes his/her utility or profit and then shows that an equilibrium is achieved which guarantees a maximum efficiency. Management, on the other side, especially quantitative methods, provided me with devices to maximize utility and profit. What people have to do is neither to suppress their instinct nor to make sacrifices but to maximize their interest, following their instinct. Fascinated by the two subjects, I came to believe that international trade law should be based on economic principles.

Since international trade, with all the importance, is ever growing and ever-changing, it is urgent to establish a sound legal system concerning trade. I would like to take part in forming a legal system based on economic principles. That, in the other side, will have another meaning to me.

In my department in my university, there were only five females out of 240 students. I usually heard the question, "What are you girls doing here in the business department?" In my country, business is still a male-dominated field let alone international trade. I hardly see female business leaders nor female lawyers, not to mention female business lawyers. Most of women students in my department, though brave to choose business as their major subject, are not brave enough to pursue a career in such a women-barren field as international trade. Getting a job in a field with less discrimination and prejudice against women may be a safe choice but not a constructive choice. What we should do is to pioneer a new field, to prove equal ability between men and women, and to extend the border of he safe area rather than to stay inside the border.

To become an international business lawyer may be rewarding for everybody but especially for me since I believe in promotion of international trade, I am a person who will contribute to establishing trade law based on economic principles, and I will be another role model for female professionals.

Strengths

The candidate's interests and goals are clear. The essay is well structured.

Weaknesses

The fact that English is a second language to the applicant becomes very clear because the essay is full of grammatical errors. She has good things to say in the essay but would have benefited greatly from an editing service that enabled her to express her thoughts more eloquently.

ESSAY 17: Interest in Law and Technology; Active in Model UN

When the federal agents arrived early that morning, my friend Adam didn't have a chance. They took everything during the raid—every piece of computer-related equipment he owned, from disks to telephone cords. Adam, a competent "hacker," never did tell me that day's entire sequence of events, but I knew enough to realize that his life was changed forever. This was my first encounter with the law, and at the impressionable age of fourteen, I was affected.

Perhaps, then, my initial interest in the law arose out of fear for my own safety: I wanted to be certain that whatever I did with my computer was legal. Irrespective of the motivation, I began to ask questions and read about computer laws. To my amazement, I found little material. Over the next few years, it occurred to me that advancing technology was opening doors that society, armed with its laws, was ill-equipped to enter. This grew more apparent as outrageous anecdotes became prevalent in the media: computer failures in surgery, police arrests based on erroneous data, privacy invasion. While I continued to research the consequential dilemmas, I pondered their solutions and even published some articles. During these years, I saw the public begin to confront these dilemmas as well. Debate among philosophers, academians, scientists, and lawmakers swelled, and then I understood: this was the dynamic, evolutionary nature of the law. Issues were emerging; ideas were forming. Society was responding.

When I matriculated in 1988, the engineering school at [school] did not offer a course which addressed the societal implications of advancing technology. During my sophomore year I approached a professor and we eventually created and taught such a course together. The class was a unique approach to education: we held roundtable discussions with guest speakers who were experts in this relatively young field, including Mitch Kapor (founder of Lotus and the EFF), Jerry Berman (former ACLU lawyer), and Marc Rotenberg (founder of Computer Professionals for Social Responsibility). Through this class, my view of the law broadened. I saw how well-intentioned laws can be misused against people, even by the government. I witnessed how the absence of law and its framework for order and justice can be devastating. Most importantly, I realized that constructing the law in response to a dilemma can be a slow and difficult process because there may be no clear answers, especially when the dilemma is not fully understood. Nonetheless, I saw that I could apply my problem-solving, reasoning, and writing skills in constructing preliminary solutions.

My interest in this form of problem-solving extended beyond just technology issues. I found the intellectual process so exhilarating that I was eager to engage it with respect to other dilemmas that concerned me. Consequently, I joined the model United Nations organization at [school]. As chairman of a committee of about one hundred delegates, I researched, wrote papers, and moderated discussions on terrorism, Antarctic exploitation, Latin American economic unity, and drug legalization; I chose these topics because of their timeliness, their significance, their diversity, and their interest to me. Our debates were sometimes more educational and more practical than classroom learning. In fact, grappling with these issues forced us to think outside of academia. We witnessed the need for negotiation and compromise, and we often constructed innovative solutions. More importantly, we participated in a process that identified, confronted, and attempted to resolve societal dilemmas. I have participated in very few experiences which were as satisfying to me as these.

Lawmakers define how society will deal with complex issues. They contribute lasting improvements to the structure which governs society by addressing those issues which undermine society. It is my desire to actively participate in this process, and I believe that law school will be the beginning of a new education which will equip me with the necessary mental tools to attain my goals.

Strengths

The essay is very well written and well structured. It is interesting and it is unveiled in an effective format. Beginning with a story sparks immediate interest. The story provides a great transition to the applicant's motivation to study law. The applicant's motivations are then backed up through his experiences, which also provide some evidence that he will make a good lawyer. The applicant comes across as intelligent, motivated, and qualified.

Weaknesses

None.

ESSAY 18: International Background; Career Switcher; Financial Consultant and CPA; Religious Volunteer; Tax Law Experience

My background and upbringing include the countries of Germany, Indonesia, Singapore, Russia, China, Brazil, Thailand, Taiwan and Iran. In 1953, my German father, who grew up in Indonesia and Singapore, met my Russian mother onboard a passenger liner. She was fleeing her hometown of Shanghai to seek stability in Brazil after Mao Tse Tung won control of China. After marrying, my parents worked in Thailand, where my sister was born. Three years later they transferred to Taiwan, where I was born in 1968. Many years later, I married a Persian woman, adding a Middle Eastern flavor to our family's predominately European-Asian background.

This international diversity and my global travels have cultivated my unique and sensitive understanding of and appreciation for different peoples, cultures, beliefs and laws. I have become accustomed to this variety; therefore, I still travel extensively and live in a multicultural, ethnically diverse community.

At the age of sixteen, I graduated from high school and started college. To help finance my education, I worked full-time at a bank and then throughout my junior and senior years, three nights a week at a restaurant. During my free time I actively involved myself with Beta Alpha Psi, the national honorary accounting society. As their Alumni Relations Officer, I organized the "CPA for a Day" annual program, scheduled guest speakers for special events and distributed students' resumes to hiring firms. In addition, I participated each year in the school's Volunteer Income Tax Assistance program.

Four years later, at the age of twenty, I was proud to have graduated with highest honors in business administration (99th percentile for [school] graduates applying to law schools), especially considering my twenty-hour a week work schedule, campus activities and rigorous academic curriculum. These facts demonstrate that I consistently achieve academic success, despite the challenges presented.

During the fall semester of 1988, I accepted a general management consulting job with one of the big six accounting firms in Los Angeles. This was a unique accomplishment because consultant positions had in prior years required a graduate degree or doctorate. During the next three years, I acquired a Certified Public Accountant license and earned a promotion to become the firm's youngest senior consultant. Management valued and praised my consistent success in a variety of projects, such as market research, financial analysis, strategic planning, sales training, software testing, auditing and tax work. In retrospect, I recognize that these business experiences created a strong foundation for legal studies. General consulting developed strategizing, critical thinking, interviewing and oral speaking skills. Auditing advanced my ability to find numerical and statistical inconsistencies, and cultivated skills similar to those necessary for discovering flaws in legal argumentation. (Please see my enclosed resume.)

Much of my personal time has involved various nondenominational Christian ministries and church activities. For instance, I helped organize a Christian household of seven roommates, where five of us cared for two people dying from AIDS-related illnesses. I also participated in numerous organized and individual efforts to supply food and clothing for the homeless. These commitments provided me with the opportunities to assist people from all backgrounds and to give something back to the community. In addition, I volunteered my accounting skills to help members of my church prepare their tax returns and to provide financial advice. After assisting one member understand various financial and legal options in a budgetary crisis, I began to realize my personal interest in practicing law. Becoming an attorney will give me a long-term opportunity for work that is not only intellectually challenging but also offers me the privilege of helping others. To confirm my interest in law, I obtained employment as a financial analyst with a nationally recognized law firm specializing in municipal finance.

During the following three years, I have advanced my knowledge of municipal finance and applicable tax law under the direction of two attorneys. I have found my capacity for absorbing the ever-changing federal treasury regulations to be excellent and the work to be challenging and enriching. Each year the tax attorneys have given me increased responsibilities, including the training of other analysts and assistants, and the final review of all complex financial reports and analyses. (Please see my enclosed resume)

I now know firsthand that practicing law entails long hours, hard work, self-discipline and total commitment. My successful business career has shown that I have this commitment, which I plan to leverage with my financial expertise and CPA license to succeed as an attorney.

In summary, I will bring maturity, determination and seriousness of purpose to my legal studies. In addition, my multicultural background, extensive professional experience and community service involvement will contribute uniquely to the diversity of the [university] School of Law.

Strengths

The essay is effective because the candidate manages to include many academic, work, and general life experiences that portray him as an intelligent and qualified applicant who will no doubt succeed in law school. He does so in a well-structured essay that covers many of the basic topics that admissions committees like addressed: motivation, experience, qualifications, and how a law degree will enhance the applicant's career.

Weaknesses

The candidate refers to his resume twice—this should never be done. Despite the fact that it is generally well written, the essay still contains grammatical errors.

ESSAY 19: Activist Since Childhood; Student Body President

At the age of eighteen, I never expected to receive so much attention. After two years of trying to persuade the local Scout council to abandon its widespread use of the Confederate battle flag, my letter to the National Office paid off. Newspapers nationwide reported that my letter spurred the Boy Scouts of America to issue a policy restricting use of the flag. As a conservative white Southerner whose family moved here in 1635, I had to explain that this policy was not just politically correct, but that it made sense.

Nine years ago, I was inducted into the Order of the Arrow (OA), a selective Scout organization designed to encourage leadership and community service. My seventy-member induction class included twenty black Scouts, but I never saw more than one or two of them at OA events. I became concerned that the OA was not developing leaders from one-third of our state's population, and wondered why blacks returned so rarely. I remembered the pervasiveness of the Confederate flag on induction weekend—decorating mugs and T-shirts, hanging from flagpoles and in the dining hall. While I knew the flag was not the root cause of the problem, I decided that its removal would help keep black Scouts in the OA.

Therefore, as editor of the regional OA newsletter, I published an article critical of the flag. Several black Scouts quietly confirmed my suspicions. One Scout recalled that his mother, seeing the flags in the camp dining hall, pulled him aside and whispered, "I don't think we're welcome here." More typical was the response of a prominent Scout leader, who angrily demanded to know why any debate was even necessary since "we only have two blacks in the lodge anyway." I could not believe how thoroughly he had missed my point.

Though my local efforts were thwarted, I still believed that Scouting should abandon the flag. One year later, my letter to the National Office prompted the new policy and ignited a storm of public debate. Critics blasted my disrespect for Southern tradition, misinterpreting my desire to help the South as an apology for the Civil War. I am proud of my relatives who fought and died for the Confederacy, but it is not their image that the flag represents when it is used at twentieth century Scout meetings, football games, and NASCAR races. Scouts began using the flag in the 1950s, about the time Georgia and South Carolina raised it over their State Houses. The flag is a response to unpopular Supreme Court justices, not invading armies.

Ironically, [school's] student newspaper has charged that I lack compassion and only represent white male fraternity members on a fraternity-dominated campus. The newspaper did not endorse me for student body president because I refused to give unconditional support to every cause, including de-emphasis of Western curricula and mandatory hiring quotas for black faculty. The editors downplayed my leading role in establishing the first main campus housing for a black fraternity, a woman's selective group, and a multicultural organization, because they believed that the fraternities should have been kicked off campus instead. Nonetheless, I was the first person to be elected without their endorsement in twenty years because students recognized my commitment to the entire community.

The battle flag has slowly disappeared from Scouting, and [school's] campus better reflects the school's diversity. While integration is still a distant goal, these changes are small steps in the right direction. I sought practical improvements through independent thinking, perseverance, and tenacity in the face of fierce criticism. A legal education would give me tools to better use these abilities. I am not headed to law school on a mission, but I see law as an opportunity to contribute as we build our future.

Strengths

This essay is well written and interesting. It is very effective because it demonstrates the applicant's strengths and motivations through his actions, not his words. He does not bore the reader by simply stating why he is qualified and where his interests lie—he lets his experiences unveil it all.

Weaknesses

None.

ESSAY 20: Influence of Book; Personal Change; Vietnamese; Family Background; Philosophy Major

"How many a man has dated a new era in his life from the reading of a book." (Thoreau)

One evening, during Christmas vacation of my freshman year in college, when a formidable storm outside called for an evening of hot tea and heavy reading, I picked up a book that had been sitting on my desk for several weeks. On the cover, it read "Selections of the Essays: Montaigne." On the inside, only a few circled page numbers evidenced that the book had ever been used.

I was supposed to have read Montaigne that past quarter for Honors Humanities Core, but had, instead, done no more than to skim key pages highlighted in lecture—enough to earn myself a decent grade in the course.

That was how I approached school then—with the goal of getting the highest possible grade with the least possible effort. Grades have always been, after all, very important to me. Having been unsure as to what I wanted to do in life, I figured that getting good grades would insure that once I decided on what I wanted, that that opportunity would still lie open for me. Such, then, was how I justified my attitude towards studying; it served the very practical goal of rendering myself "marketable."

This approach to academics is not original. My parents taught me that the only way I would get anywhere in life (in the States) was through education. United States immigrants, arriving in 1975 as refugees from Vietnam, our family was forced to leave all our belongings behind. We had to make a fresh start in a foreign country. My father's only asset was his mind—he had a college education. The first five years we were here, he worked at a sewage plant while studying on his own for the country's engineering exam. After passing the exam, he got a job as a civil engineer at the City of Anaheim. Six years later, he was promoted to a position above that of his own boss, then,—that of Water Engineering Manager. All along, what he taught my four siblings and I was that the best thing we could do for ourselves was to study hard. Education (along with hard work), he always said, serve as the key to succeeding and to earning people's respect in this country (which he did). I still believe him, but I have since learned that such practical ends are not the *sole* purpose of education.

I opened the book that evening, curious as to what I might have missed in my efforts to minimize the quarter's workload, and found more. I found myself in the middle of Montaigne's essay "On the Education of Children." Emerson once wrote that "within books, the good reader finds confidences, or asides, hidden from all else and unmistakably meant for his ear. The profoundest thought or passion sleeps as if in a mind until it is discovered by an equal mind and heart." Such was my encounter with philosophy that evening. Montaigne's words did not claim some vacant chair inside my mind, as if at an auction, hoping to win its bid for my attention. They pounced on me, rather, drilled deep into my core, and dragged out gems I had long buried. "The first lessons in which we should steep [a student's] mind," I read, "must be those that regulate his behavior and his sense, that will teach him to know himself and to die well and to live well." Montaigne's words did not so much teach me anything new, as they reminded me of beliefs I had once held, of ideas I had previously known, but forgotten or discarded as childish and impractical.

That book, read numerous times since, served as a catalyst for both my personal and academic growth. Montaigne inspired me to stress the attainment of wisdom over the acquisition of knowledge. I used to study enough to gather the "facts" of a theory, my essays having been not much more than reports on those facts, perhaps, frosted over with a bit of commentary. I tasted ideas, chewed on them for as long as it took to take my tests, and then spit them out. They did not change me but for a brief grin at a pleasant idea or a wrinkling of the nose at a bitter one. I told myself that it would be a waste of time to try and fully absorb any of the material I was studying, much less form an opinion on it. I made a mistake, then, that I had promised myself years before never to make. I became so worried about preparing a living, that I forgot to make a life for myself. For while my grades were thriving, my mind was stagnating. I did not grow; I did not change.

I changed my major, then, from Social Science to Philosophy, so that I might "study *myself* more than any other subject," to make, as Montaigne said, "*that* . . . my metaphysics; that . . . my physics." I wanted to learn not just for the grade, nor even for knowledge, itself—not just to impress strangers at a cocktail party or friends over coffee by being able to toss out names of ancient philosophers, or current celebrities, and their theories. I wanted, instead, to savor what was in the world—to take from books and people their views, to sample them, digest them, to make some my own, to reject others, and to store some away for further consideration. I wanted to become something more—someone better—for what I had studied, or for whom I had met.

Looking back on these past years as a philosophy major, I am only a little embarrassed at not being able to recall the name of an certain author, or the term for a specific idea. By the time I graduate, I may actually have forgotten the majority of those "facts" learned throughout my college career. This, however, does not concern me too much. To succeed externally, to mechanically be able to repeat information, is one thing, but to be able to say that you have created something internally, that you have made something more of yourself, means so much more. As Matthew Arnold wrote, "Life is not a having and a getting, but a being and becoming." To be able to color my thoughts with others' ideas, and yet, blend them into a pattern that is mine alone: that, to me, is the ultimate end of education.

Strengths

This is a unique, interesting, and well-written essay. The reader gets to know a little about the personality of the applicant through his discussion of education and how its meaning has changed to him over the years. It is different enough to stand out and to hold the attention of the reader. Because it is so well written, and because it has much to do with the importance of education to the applicant, he comes across as intelligent and as a candidate who will likely succeed in law school.

Weaknesses

The essay would have been more effective if the applicant had tied in anything about law school. Whether it was his motivation for studying law or what he planned to do with the law degree, any tidbit would have made the essay more relevant. It is good enough to stand on its own, but if he had seamlessly integrated some information on how the study of law fits into his life, the essay would have been outstanding.

ESSAY 21: Black; Moderate Liberal; Republican Convention
Stranger in a Strange Land: Validating An Ideological Commitment

What the hell am I doing? This question recurred frequently as I made the two hour drive from Stanford to Sacramento. Even turning the stereo up so loud I could hear my vents rattle didn't distract me for long. My fixation should have been no surprise. Had I told most of my friends where I intended to spend the next two days I would have been answered with vacuous eyes and gaping mouths. I had agreed to attend a convention that was being held way out in Sacramento. What was unusual was that I was attending a convention of the California College Republicans.

I do not mean to suggest that there is anything inherently wrong with the G.O.P., but it simply has never been my cup of tea. Back in elementary school I accepted that the Republicans were running the country (via the White House) and doing a deplorable job of it. Before I understood what party identification was all about I knew the words Reagan and Bush and came to identify these names with all of the major inequities and plights of America. The problem of race relations were caused by Republican insensitivity, as were the problems of poverty, poor education and the threat of nuclear war. The government was an old conservative beast that was apathetic to the difficulties of the under-privileged. That was the setting in which I grew up and even as I undertook the eternal drive to Sacramento I could not escape the oppressive feeling that I was betraying my past. How did I get to this point?

I guess it all started back in high school. All those years of private schooling can have a profound effect on a person's attitude. Sure, I was used to cheering the liberal cause and disdaining any hint of conservatism, but it was the trendy thing to do. Western Massachusetts was a place where everyone, Blacks, Whites, Latinos, homosexuals, poor, wealthy, even those afflicted with AIDS, seemed to get along okay. It never seemed idealistic that a multicultural and tolerant America was a coveted possibility.

I soon realized that I was developing opinions that were inconsistent with my claimed ideology. Back in 1991 the specter of Clarence Thomas brought the concept of a black conservative to national attention and it was not received well. Yet in spite of how ardently I joined the criticism, I found myself agreeing with some of what he had to say. Maybe affirmative action is being carried to a harmful extreme, and maybe a lot of people spend too much time looking for scapegoats instead of accepting primary responsibility for their own unfortunate situation. Regardless, what was clear over my college years was that even though the labels Democrat and Republican were on opposite sides of my spectrum of virtue, my own views were not so easily categorized.

My sophomore year in college I was engaged in a conversation surrounding the recent presidential election and a student reacted with surprise when I mentioned that I supported Clinton. She thought I was a Republican because I spent most of my time hanging around people who were. I was stunned. The last thing I ever wanted was for anyone to guess that I endorsed the Republican party or anything it stood for. I have often heard Republicans say to me that my opinions are not all as liberal as I think and that there was room for me under the G.O.P.'s "big tent." I heard those remarks so often that they eventually began to lose their shock value. Yet always, I was content in my belief that I was, undeniably, a true liberal. But after some tumultuous ideological clashes in college I wound up among friends who were active in the college Republican cause and sought to drag me in.

The prospect of attending this convention was unappealing, but the truth was I had nothing better to do that Friday night. Besides, I needed to clarify to myself that even though I had shifted slightly to the right in recent years, I had not made a complete turn around. So I packed a bag, put on a suit (I couldn't help expressing my liberal slant, I wore a lavender shirt with a black and purple tie) and headed into the lion's den.

For the first time in my life I felt like a foreigner in America. I walked into the hotel lobby and a huge banner circumnavigated the far wall like a frieze reading: "Doing time in San Clinton . . . 836 days until parole!" I came across people who wore buttons reading: "Rush Limbaugh in

'96," "Clinton-Gore, out in four!" and "Hillary free zone." At one point the entire convention was howling madly after hearing a speech written by Patrick Buchanan. Later everyone around me rose and saluted a slide projection of Ronald Reagan sitting in the Oval Office. All I could think of was what my English teacher during my senior year of high school once said: "the nice thing about right-wingers is they always fulfill your worst expectations of them."

The most harrowing aspect of the convention was the awkwardness that accompanied me wherever I went. As I walked around I felt like a novelty. I was one of only four black students there (none female). Normally this would mean nothing to me but suddenly I became aware of the homogeneity of the assembly. People often complain about feeling indoctrinated by multiculturalism or political correctness in college, but I actually began to miss those institutions. Sure, I normally am indifferent to the racial composition of a social function, but I generally do not feel suspicious of anyone's predetermined attitude toward me. How could I feel at home amongst a subculture whose rhetoric stereotypes me as a violent criminal, welfare abuser, drug addict, or beneficiary of undeserved educational opportunity? You can only put on a happy face for so long before the sideways glances and whispers as you roam the halls begin to weigh on your conscience. At one point some student running for a California Republicans elected position gave a speech in which he began "I am pro-family, I oppose abortion, I am pro-gun and I am anti-expansion of rights for sodomites." My first reaction? I was inclined to scream at this thick headed neo-nazi and ask him if he had been to any good cross burnings lately. But then I reflected carefully on the situation. Maybe tolerance means I have to stomach the opinions of people who make me nauseous. Maybe, just maybe if I dislike what I have seen and heard throughout the weekend then I am the one who simply does not belong. Maybe my convictions have been correct all along; the Republican party is not for me.

I left the convention before the major event had taken place: the election of College Republican officers. Interestingly that was why my friends wanted me there. The more bodies they had representing Stanford, the more votes they could cast in their favor. Since I hated the experience and I left before I could make good on the favor I promised, I wondered, what had I gained?

I was obsessed with this enigma on the way home. I had driven more than two hours to be somewhere I had no desire to go and interact with people I had no desire to meet. On top of all of that I had a paper due the next day in a seminar and had not even started working on it. After the two hour drive back I would have roughly forty-five minutes before I had to go to work at the library, which for me always signaled the end of my weekend. These definitely were not the most fun and productive two days of my life.

But somehow I felt a hint of satisfaction or maybe even a bit of relief. At least I better understood why my political identification was appropriate. I hated masquerading as a conservative Republican, not just because I had to deceive people who were polite to me, but also because I was denying myself. Deep down I firmly believe that some degree of affirmative action short of imposing quotas is necessary to unfreeze status quo and remedy the effects of past discrimination. I believe that women cannot be equal to men in society until they are granted full reproductive rights and we cease capitalist exploitation based on gender that pervades workplaces and homes. I believe that the equal protection clause of the Fourteenth Amendment means that it is unconstitutional for anyone to discriminate against another person based on his/her sexual orientation in the realm of employment, housing and public accommodations. I believe that the taking of human life is unjust even if exacted as a punishment by a law enforcement agency. I firmly believe in the strict separation of church and state, so much so that I would take the words "in God we trust" off of all U.S. currency. I also believe that, in the post–Cold War era, national welfare concerns should take precedence over international primacy aspirations. Now, if after all of that there may still be a place for me in the Republican party, I am eager to find out where.

My commitment to these beliefs was immersed in hostility while I attended the convention but it guided me through the event. I tried something new and simply did not like it. My clearest recollection from the whole weekend is the gorgeous sunshine as I drove back to Stanford and the exhilaration I felt as I put more and more distance between me and that hotel. I was proud of myself. I now knew that clashing with conservative dogma was not just something I did to fit into left leaning social situations, it was essential to the identity I have developed since childhood. I know myself to fit the description of an emphatically moderate liberal. I could associate with staunch conservatives while I maintained a separate and contrasting ideological posture. I was brave enough to test the strength of personal beliefs and leave confidently and calmly. It was a sullen, quiet time as I drove back to Stanford, yet the ride back didn't seem to take very long.

Strengths

This is a very interesting essay that reveals much about the applicant through his political beliefs and his willingness to try things out of his comfort zone. It is actually fun to read because it is written with such passion and is different from the typical application essay. The applicant comes across as very intelligent and his perceived activism (through his intense discussion of politics) gives the impression that he will be a very active participant in the law school classroom and in other campus and community activities.

Weaknesses

The essay is far too long, not because it ever loses the attention of the reader, but because it extends too far beyond the requested word limits. While it is easy to envision this applicant in law school, and frankly it seems like a natural fit, the applicant never makes a direct reference to it in the essay. This applicant may have gotten away with it, but applicants in general should be careful of expressing their beliefs *too* strongly because they run the risk of offending someone on the admissions committee.

ESSAY 22: Honors Program; Supplemental Instructor; Community Service

I entered [school] with over 100 credit hours that I had earned from Advanced Placement Tests and the Governor's Honors Academy. This presented me with the options of graduating with a bachelor's degree in less than two years, or taking advantage of the entire four years of my scholarship and using the surplus hours to participate in either intellectual or extracurricular activities that I might otherwise not have time for. As my transcript reflects, I chose the latter of these options, and that has been one of the best choices I have ever made. Using the extra time to enroll in the University Honors Program and to serve in various leadership capacities, my college career has been one of tremendous personal growth and service to others.

The Honors Program has been an important part of my intellectual development. With small classes composed of professors and students that are serious about education, the Honors Program encourages a cooperative learning environment that stresses analysis and reasoning. Furthermore, the topics offered by the program are as diverse as my own interests. Ranging from constitutional law to pharmacology to philosophy, the courses all involved extensive reading and placed emphasis on developing verbal and written communication skills. As a result, my education has focused on developing critical thinking skills, not memorizing.

Beyond furthering my education, my college years have also allowed me to act on my belief that individuals have a responsibility to contribute to their communities. I have had the opportunity to help empower others through a variety of activities, but two merit special mention. The first is my involvement as a Supplemental Instructor for the past three years. The Supplemental Instruction Program is designed to get successful undergraduates involved in the education of other undergraduates. The program chooses two students from each discipline each year to act as peer leaders in introductory level courses. The Supplemental Instructor conducts three class or discussion sessions each week designed to help the students succeed in the course, develop a more thorough understanding of the course material through discussions, and to empower them to succeed throughout the remainder of their college careers by sharing study skills and learning strategies. My involvement has not only helped others learn, but also has taught me valuable lessons in dealing with people from diverse racial, ethnic, and educational backgrounds.

The Residence Hall Student Association (RHSA) also allowed me to use my leadership abilities to impact others' lives. The two most important contributions the RHSA makes are to organize and promote community service projects and to plan education and social events. As vice president of the organization, I spearheaded such diverse community service activities as a fund raiser for the university library, an "Into the Streets" week of neighborhood service projects, recording textbooks onto audio tapes for blind students, and a "Project Youth" day of linking college students with underprivileged junior high school students to emphasize the importance of a college education. In addition to community service projects, I also planned educational and social events for the residents. The events ranged from programs concerned with time management, study skills, and campus rape to activities such as a formal ball and murder mystery to a spring carnival. Motivating students to get involved in community service and helping promote individual growth through various programs transformed my experience in the RHSA from one of simple leadership to one of personal fulfillment.

In retrospect, my decision to take full advantage of my college years enabled me to learn invaluable lessons. The combination of teaching experience, leadership experiences, and community services activities greatly enriched my life, expanding my view of the world and deepening my understanding of how people think and behave. I would not trade those years for any "jump-start" on my career. Besides, who would really want to hire a 22-year-old lawyer anyway?

Strengths

The essay is straightforward and easy to read. It is a standard application essay that includes recent achievements and paints the picture of a well-rounded and motivated student.

Weaknesses

The essay could have been stronger if the applicant had revealed more of her personality by telling a story from her college experience instead of discussing only achievements. The applicant also could have revealed her motivation for attending law school.

ESSAY 23: Community College; Model UN Teaching Assistant; Politically Active

One way to give you a sense of who I am is to explain how and why I co-founded the Norrie Point Model United Nations Program and Project Engagement, two educational initiatives for high school students in Dutchess County, NY. These initiatives are one way in which the unusual trajectory of my undergraduate career, led to positive and productive ends. They illustrate some of the personal qualities which help make me a strong candidate for admission to [law school].

When I attended Community College, I served briefly as a political columnist for the school newspaper. I enjoyed the writing but grew increasingly discouraged by the widespread political disengagement of my peers. Try as I might, I could not illicit reader response. There was little appetite for political activity and virtually no shared sense of social responsibility. With some exceptions, community leadership by students was an anathema. When I graduated and crossed town to attend [college]—where students regularly volunteer at local schools, soup kitchens, women's shelters, health clinics and mentoring programs—my discouragement inspired action.

By my experience in local high schools, which constitute [school] feeder community, I knew that most students were taught politics by rote and without enthusiasm. In that way politics were the same as algebra. Either you prospered by native interest or you memorized what you needed to know and got by. Naturally, this approach did not teach civic responsibility or foster political engagement; if anything, it bred generalized apathy. But Professor of Government Richard Reitano, who became my partner in both the Norrie Point and Project Engagement endeavors, taught me that educators could engage students in political thought. His Model United Nations program at [school] prepares student delegations to the National Model United Nations in New York City. I participated in this program. It was my introduction to the use of simulation as a teaching tool and ultimately became a model for the Norrie Point program.

After I transferred to [college], I became a Teaching Assistant in the Model United Nations program. I returned to [school] once a week to lecture, review position papers, critique practice speeches and coach delegates. Professor R. and I began developing a productive and special working relationship. We often discussed the classroom difficulties he faced as his students—the products of local high schools—increasingly failed to grasp the equation of citizenship with political engagement and civic responsibility. We were optimistic, however, that we could get local students excited about politics. What they needed was a program which employed creative and highly interactive teaching methods; a program which gave the political process the human face it lacked.

Our idea was to gather hundreds of students from local high-schools and conduct one-day model United Nations simulations. These simulations would require students to study and debate policy solutions to international political issues such as the disintegration of Somalia or the threat posed to peace and security by North Korea's nuclear weapons program. But the "issues" were really secondary. Our goal was to foster political engagement in area kids by turning them into would be policy-makers.

In 1994 we conducted two model United Nations simulations at Norrie Point, an educational center on the Hudson River in Hyde Park, NY. Buoyed by the success of these two events, we founded Project Engagement. This new initiative incorporated the goals and lessons of the Norrie Point program but was not limited to the model United Nations format. The first Project Engagement forum, which dealt with the future of United States immigration policy, was held at [school] last November.

The Norrie Point and Project Engagement initiatives were well received in the educational community. Faculty from area high-schools indicated that the programs often had a quantifiable effect on the overall academic performance of the participants. In several instances students applied to take part in future simulations, even without knowledge of which issues would be addressed. Others told me that the simulations were critical points in their high-school careers, and that they had decided to study Political Science as undergraduates. Three students who participated in the first Norrie Point program are attending [school] this year. Each has applied and been admitted to Professor R.'s National Model United Nations program.

Perhaps it would have been expedient to downplay my time at community college. But Norrie Point and Project Engagement were created because of—not despite —my unusual undergraduate career. I am proud of my role in both initiatives, but am also ready to put them aside and pursue my legal education. The lessons I take from Norrie Point and Project Engagement are, however, applicable in any challenging situation. Each required substantial time, focus and preparation. I had to learn by doing. I made mistakes but recovered. Through partnership and hard work I helped turn a good idea into a meaningful reality.

The Norrie Point Model United Nations Program and Project Engagement demonstrate that I am capable of significant initiative. However, success at [name of law school] and in my professional life will not come through initiative alone. I am a discerning, creative and diligent student. I endeavor to be ethical and socially responsible in thought and in behavior. I thrive on challenges and I am optimistic enough to believe in taking risks if they will help me or those I care about grow. I believe these qualities enable me for success at [name of law school].

Strengths

The essay is strong because the applicant demonstrates initiative and activism through her experiences, not through a discussion of achievements. She succeeds in her attempt to change the perception of attending community college as a weak point in her academic career to one that helped her grow and ultimately achieve greater success as a student.

Weaknesses

The introduction is forced. She could have eliminated the first paragraph altogether, which would have helped her reduce the overall length in addition to deleting unnecessary material.

ESSAY 24: Career Switcher; Engineer; Teacher

"Where did we go wrong?" were the first words offered by my mechanical engineering professor when I told him I wanted to go to law school. Nearly everyone I have spoken to has had something bad to say about the career choice. Somehow, despite all the jokes, criticism, and quotations from Shakespeare, my commitment to attend law school has remained strong.

My career as an engineer began when I qualified for the cooperative education program (co-op) as a freshman at [school]. As a co-op, I alternated between school and work every semester, including the summer sessions. The co-op program was a great opportunity. Not only did I benefit from the full-time work experience, but my salary also enabled me to manage nearly all of my educational expenses. Unfortunately, the stress of the unusual schedule and change of role every semester had a negative impact on my grades. As I adjusted to the process, however, my annual grade point average improved from 3.15 to 3.57.

I was able to dedicate my time to academics after I completed the co-op program. In a required course, the Aircraft Corporation asked all seniors to propose a solution to a design problem. My group spent eight weeks analyzing and solving the problem before we gave our presentation. It was a huge success. After we navigated through a barrage of questions, Aircraft Corporation selected our proposal as the best of all those presented. At the same time, I took 5 courses, two of which were graduate level, and performed research in [school's] combustion and optics laboratories. As a result of my research, I co-authored an article that was published by the Institute to aid in the prevention of uncontrolled oil well fires.

Graduating a semester ahead of schedule, I returned to work for [name of company]. I stayed there until I reached my five year service anniversary and then relocated to Boston. Moving over 1,000 miles across the country alone was quite a challenge and the contrast between my small town upbringing and life in a large city has definitely increased my self-confidence and social awareness.

Besides enjoying the diverse culture and activities of Boston, I have studied classical guitar, rediscovered my artistic ability by preparing drawings for exhibit, explored the culinary arts, and found an interest in classic poetry. After a few discussions with my guitar instructor, he went so far as to give me the name, "renaissance man." Though my activities have covered a wide range of topics, I found that they have one common element. They all require persistence and attention to detail, qualities that will undoubtedly be helpful in law school.

I began to seriously consider furthering my education last fall. I applied to a number of schools to pursue a doctorate in engineering and began investigating the possibility of attending law school. My end goal was to become a professor, regardless of the discipline I would choose. This desire was partially due to the satisfaction I felt when I helped my fellow students in class at [school]. It was also influenced by teaching science to elementary school students in a volunteer program sponsored by [name of company] called, *Wheels in Motion*.

I wrestled with the decision of which subject to pursue until the following spring. In May, University presented me with a fully funded offer to attend graduate school as a teaching assistant. It was a once in a lifetime offer, but after careful consideration I decided that I would prefer teaching and writing about the law and respectfully declined.

My decision to turn down the scholarship was not easy, but my research into law school made it evident that I had made the right choice. Besides reading books about law school and talking with lawyers about their careers, I visited nearly a half dozen campuses and attended a seminar hosted in Washington, D. C. by a number of law professors from around the country. Talking with the professors at the seminar, attending law classes, and my experience with academic publication at University reinforced my decision to pursue a career as a professor of law.

I took nearly an entire year to make my decision to attend law school. It was based upon a career goal that was developed through both research and experience. I have a background that will add a unique perspective to classroom discussions, a successful academic career, and the maturity to realize my goals. I believe that I have demonstrated not only a sincere and well-founded commitment to pursue a law degree, but also the ability and desire to be successful in this pursuit.

Strengths

In this essay, the applicant briefly and successfully explained a weak point in his application. He does not whine about it or harp on it, but offers a legitimate reason for a low GPA early in his college experience. He integrates this subject very well into the other essay topics. He also briefly discusses some new experiences since college that offer the reader a little more insight into his personality. He also answers the questions of why he wants to attend law school and what he wants to do with the degree.

Weaknesses

Although this may not be one of the most interesting personal statements out there, it does not have any real weaknesses. It is effective and successfully achieves the goals of an application essay.

ESSAY 25: Sailing; Overcoming an Obstacle

Having long wanted to learn to sail, I joined the crew of the US Brig Niagara last summer. Based in Erie, Pennsylvania, the two masted tall ship requires a large crew of professionals and volunteers to perform maintenance and sailing duties. I soon discovered that much of my time on board would be spent washing dishes, scrubbing decks, and hauling lines. My work in the ship's rigging, however, presented me with major challenges. I will carry what I achieved from meeting those challenges in many of my future endeavors.

I picked a choppy and gusty day for my first trip aloft to help unfurl sails. Immediately, I discovered that peering down from a platform 80 feet above deck robbed me of all my normal faculties. The vertigo that had long plagued me whenever I ventured too near the edge of some precipice or too high into a tree had caught up to me in the rigging. Queasiness quickly replaced my disappointment at this discovery, however. Spotting my heaving chest and buckling legs, my petty officer, Mark, immediately ordered me back to deck.

I tried going aloft again on a day of calm wind and still waters. Under Mark's supervision, I climbed back into the rigging and inched my way out onto a yardarm. Struggling to control my labored breathing, I attempted to focus on the job at hand so I could climb quickly off the toothpick-like timber. No matter that I was "roped in" with a safety harness, I was still rendered completely ineffective by my surroundings.

During one of my next trips aloft, I found it possible to recover some control once I forced the shudders to retreat from my body. When I paused to analyze my situation, I knew my vertigo would not prevent me from maneuvering safely. "Ben! Pay attention and help me furl this sail so we can get out of here," barked Mark. Visions of Bouncing Bens quickly dissipated. He reminded me that we were hanging from the yard to perform a task, not for me to reflect on the state of my phobias.

I continued to climb into the rigging, determined to master my fears enough to perform good work. On one trip onto a craneline hanging near a mast, I forced every detail concerning the location of my body and velocity of its parts to come into precise focus. My mind emptied of all else, I slowed down the task until I could gain command over each of its component parts. To help maintain control, I avoided the sensorial shock that accompanied the sight of my shoes balanced on a thin bit of line 60 feet above deck. By concentrating on the pace of my breathing and the exact position of my hands, I could almost forget that I was no longer roped in. Without any safety devices to break a fall, I was totally on my own.

One day near the end of my four weeks aboard the Niagara, I was ordered aloft by the first mate to furl a topgallant sail, one of the highest sails on the ship. Mark and I quickly finished tying down the sail. When I returned to deck, the first mate asked me how it had gone. I assured him that the ship's violent rocking had not prevented us from accomplishing the task. He looked knowingly at me for a moment before racing back to his duties. I then realized that not only had he been keeping an eye on my performances aloft, he had sent me to the topgallant yard to test my abilities. And I had told him that the work was done and done well, not that I hadn't felt too queasy or didn't catch any glimpses of my imminent demise.

I had previously transformed myself from a quivering greenhorn to a focused and concentrated amateur, trying to stay one balanced and well planned step ahead of my fears. My first mate's reaction led me to reflect that I had now achieved a level of unconscious and steady competence and was free from the need to prove or reinforce it. While I had laid the foundation for becoming a strong sailor, I had also developed a method of dismantling and controlling a major personal fear piece by piece. In the Niagara's rigging, I had found the strength and will to meet this challenge and had discovered a process for overcoming similar adversity. When I confront future obstacles, I will benefit greatly from this newfound skill.

Strengths

The author of this essay is a great writer and storyteller. It is a unique essay that most likely stood out to most admissions committees. Because the writing is so solid, it is also a testament to the applicant's overall intelligence and capacity for academic success.

Weaknesses

It is not recommended that an applicant leave any mention of law school out of his or her personal statement unless the other parts of the application are incredibly strong. That was most likely the situation here. Otherwise, it would be suggested that the applicant tie the story into his motivation for attending law school and also to end the essay with some information on what he plans to do with the degree.

ESSAY 26: Issue Analysis of Criminal Punishment; Liberal

While my undergraduate record and letters of recommendation are informative about my capacity to succeed academically in law school, I intend the following statement to reveal something about the kind of lawyer I plan to become: thoughtful, ethically oriented, and capable of developing my ideas through personal experience.

I have generally regarded vengeful approaches to punishment as ugly and barbaric. On the policy level, views that emphasize creating workable social practices have always seemed more enlightened, rational, and humane than those with the stated aim of making people suffer. On the personal level, I have regarded the retributive impulse itself—both in myself and in others—as base, irrational, and inherently illiberal. I have thought that it was necessary to choose between what I considered to be animalistic tendencies on the one hand and values such as civil libertarianism, social rationality, and compassion on the other.

Although I still feel strongly that how we punish ought to be guided far less by the idea that the guilty must pay than by considerations of general social benefit, last winter I had an experience that helped me to understand better the desire to make the guilty suffer. Furthermore, the experience caused me to question my former assumptions about the incompatibility of my vengeful feelings with my determination to act in a manner consistent with my ideals. As a result, my attitude toward my own vengeance-based impulses has changed, as have, to a lesser degree, my opinions about the proper role of victims' sentiments in criminal justice.

While vacationing with my family in Brazil, my mother, brother, and I were robbed by two bandits. At one point, one of them held a gun to my mother's head. As soon as I had a chance to collect my thoughts after this incident, I realized that I had strong feelings about what had happened to us and about the perpetrators, feelings that did not have to do with abstract considerations of policy. Instead, I was furiously angry at the thieves, and I felt that something should be done to them: not to rehabilitate them, not as a deterrent to future crime, but simply because they *deserved* it.

Still filled with these sentiments, I went with my brother that evening to the local police station to report the robbery. We looked through several books of mug shots, and found a few pictures that closely resembled the men who had robbed us. My brother suggested that we identify the closest candidates to the police, and it was then that I began to have some serious doubts. In the investigation, I wondered, what safeguards on the civil liberties of the suspects in the pictures would be employed? How could I be sure that they would receive anything like a fair trial? Of course, I was in no position to judge the integrity of these particular policemen or the adequacy of the civil liberties safeguards they customarily employed, but with reports of police massacres of Rio de Janeiro's homeless children fresh in my mind, I had some doubt as to whether even a courtroom and judge would necessarily be involved. I felt a moral obligation to consider what might happen to the people whose faces appeared in front of me, and in the end I was not willing to cooperate with the police.

The experience of being at once vengeance-driven and restrained by reason, compassion, and a concern for civil liberties has proved to be a counterexample to my former assumptions about my capacity for simultaneous reason and rage about criminal justice. Whether or not it was rational to begin with, my desire to have those men suffer remained intact. But so did my feelings born of a belief in the just treatment of criminal suspects, guilty or not. I had always assumed that allowing myself to seek retribution as a crime victim would undermine my capacity to act in accord with my values. Yet it turns out that I am capable of having vengeful sentiments that signal neither a threat to nor a retreat from my convictions.

None of this, however, convinces me that it is any more rational to wish harm upon someone for the sole reason that he or she deserves it. I have concluded only that my own inclination to feel this way is both stronger and more consistent with the dictates of my conscience than I had thought. Perhaps I am, in fact, somewhat barbaric for wanting the men to be harmed. If this is so, I am glad at least that my barbarism is not totally at odds with my liberalism.

Because of my experience in Brazil and because I know that feelings of vengeance are widely shared, I have come to be more sympathetic to the idea that it is reasonable for the criminal justice system to take into account a victim's desire for retribution. But I also feel just as strongly that in doing so it need not—and should not—forgo civil liberties safeguards. I will always believe in and argue for the civil libertarian position; moreover, I expect to be guided by it in my career as a criminal defense attorney or a legal academic. But in the future I will think twice before dismissing as readily the vengeance-driven sentiments of victims; I expect that my views, informed by experience and reflection both, will be less emotionally removed from what crime means to its victims.

Strengths

This is a fantastic personal statement for law school. It is incredibly well written, which speaks for the academic aptitude of the applicant. This essay has it all. Her motivations to attend law school are revealed in her beliefs about the criminal justice system and through the personal story that she shares. Her plans for the degree are also successfully woven into the essay's conclusion.

Weaknesses

None.

ESSAY 27: Military Background; Battery Commander; Leadership Skills

The wind shook my tent and drove the rain hard against the canvas. The walls strained against the force and my lantern swung rhythmically from the center post. November storms are not enjoyed in Washington State and my battery sought shelter for the night in the woods of Fort Lewis. That day's exercise had been a success and we settled in the best we could against the rain and cold.

I sat at the folding table that served as my desk in the field and reviewed the personnel files of Private Andrews and Specialist Richardson.

Both are good soldiers, but last week the duty officer found them drinking liquor in the barracks. It is against regulations to have alcohol in the battery area, and they were charged with a failure to follow general orders. Although this can be a substantial charge, in such matters the Army allows soldiers to waive their right to a court-martial and submit to administrative punishment. As their commander, I would decide the punishment, and I felt a little nervous as I waited for the First Sergeant to summon the two soldiers.

Two weeks before this exercise I was the Executive Officer and second-in-command of the battery. The Commander received orders for a special assignment, and three days latter I was put in charge. It is unusual for a Lieutenant to command a battery and I was surprised when the Battalion Commander gave me the job. I was excited about the challenge, but now I felt apprehensive about conducting my first disciplinary action.

The First Sergeant arrived out of the storm with the two soldiers. Andrews and Richardson reported and stood before me. I read the duty officer's statement and gave the soldiers an opportunity to explain themselves. They understood the regulations and did not dispute the charge. After conferring with the First Sergeant, I decided to restrict Specialist Richardson to the barracks with extra duty for ten days and to restrict Private Andrews for seven. I also withheld one-half of their pay for one month, but I suspended this action to encourage a return to good discipline. Specialist Richardson objected to the stiffer punishment and I used the opportunity to remind him of his responsibilities. As a senior soldier, he was expected to set a good example and to keep junior soldiers like Private Andrews out of trouble.

The next morning, I spoke to the battery at formation and reminded everyone of our current policies on alcohol and explained my position on the responsibilities of senior soldiers. I believe this incident actually proved to be good for the battery's morale and we had no more alcohol related problems that fall.

This proceeding and the seven others I conducted as a commander taught me a great deal about the power of justice. It was very rewarding to see soldiers accept just punishment, learn from their mistakes, and return to promising careers. It is now clear to me that the Law is much more than simply a system to punish offenders. Individuals can be reformed and society can overcome the transgressions of its citizens.

My experience commanding a battery in the U.S. Army has inspired me to pursue a career in the legal profession. I have always enjoyed public service and believe that I would find great satisfaction working as a prosecuting attorney or perhaps, someday, as a judge. To be accepted by an institution such as the [name of law school] would be an honor, and I now look forward to the study of law.

Strengths

This is very strong essay in which the applicant reveals a lot about himself through the personal story that he recounts. The reader gets a sense of his ethics and his stance on punishment and justice, not through his words but through his actions. Some of the applicant's strengths and achievements are also revealed, again—not through words, but through the story's revelation of his quick rise to Commander in the Army and the great responsibility that we know must have preceded his rise to this position. The essay is interesting and very well written. In the end, the applicant connects his story to his motivation to pursue a legal career. This essay contains all the components of a solid and effective personal statement.

Weaknesses

None.

ESSAY 28: Social Justice Activist; International Experience

Age 19. I was travelling by train. My destination: Refugio del Rio Grande, a cooperatively run Central American refugee camp on the Mexican border. For three months, I would be the only "outsider" living and working there. That summer, I taught English to refugees. I helped them prepare asylum applications. I sang folk songs, cooked tortillas, and drank with them. Machete in hand, I joined them in clearing fields, chopping wood, and planting corn. I listened to their narrations of political tyranny and economic subordination, and to their yearnings for change. I joined them in their attempts at democratic, communal decision-making. And at some point I stopped thinking of the refugees as "them". For a brief time, their struggle became mine, and the distinction of who was helping whom became blurred. A turning point.

Age 23. I was travelling by rental car (consciously American manufactured). My destination: River Rouge, a working-class suburb of Detroit. Map in lap, I drove in circles, my frenzied daily efforts again frustrated by a notoriously poor sense of direction. I managed to stumble upon my destination at 9:58 p.m., minutes before the nightly deadline for unannounced visits, parked and scurried to the door. This worker—my eighteenth of the day—offered several compelling reasons for not wanting to participate in a United Steelworkers' Union organizing drive. I found myself unable to even attempt an inspiring "union rap," trying instead to understand his dilemma, and leaving his home without even suggesting he sign a union card. I was not a great labor organizer.

These sketches are two examples of the various social justice-related jobs I have undertaken over the past several years. In choosing to work in diverse capacities over a range of issues, I have followed three objectives: first, to challenge my views on different problems; second, to examine the effectiveness and limitations of different strategies for affecting progressive social change; and third, to test my own aptitude, interest, and personal capacity for working in different professional roles. My attached resume thus documents a variety of issue areas (immigration, homelessness, civil rights, human rights, education, labor, and children's rights) and roles (social worker, policy analyst, researcher, teacher, community and labor organizer, and legal advocate).

As the two episodes suggest, this process revealed my interests, abilities, and limitations. Above all, several work experiences fostered an interest in law as an instrument to, and obstacle of, social change. For example, my work with the NJ Supreme Court Task Force on Minority Concerns, on a study uncovering and proposing remedies to de facto discrimination within the legal system, underlined law's potency for both perpetuating and combatting injustice. My work with the Lawyers Committee for Human Rights (LCHR) introduced me to law's potential for affecting change though creative, non-adversarial means. The results of the pilot parole project I coordinated at LCHR was cited in INS' decision to change its national policy on paroling asylum applicants.

Yet it was working for The Alliance for Children's Rights on cases of individual representation that ultimately convinced me to choose law as a vocation. As a founding staff member of the first organization in Southern California devoted exclusively to defending the legal rights of low income children, I had the opportunity to experience the excitement of creating a progressive law practice which served critical, previously unmet needs.

As Intake Coordinator, I had to quickly familiarize myself with legal areas ranging from dependency and delinquency to public benefits, family, housing, and civil rights law. As well, I developed a system for interviewing the children and assessing the cases for placement with pro bono attorneys. My relationships with the young clients gave me direct insight into the way in which law, practiced properly, can empower people to themselves take a stand against injury and injustice, and the difference this transformation makes to their self-esteem and individual fortitude.

Finally, I have tried, through my academic work, to complement action with reflection. College courses enabled me to begin grappling with broad theoretical questions of social justice, political morality, and jurisprudence. My current graduate course work in political theory is an effort to enhance my capacity to sort through these issues. I look forward to law school as a way to continue these theoretical explorations. More importantly, I am hopeful that studying law will ground the questions in a practical framework, enabling me to develop the technical skills needed to work toward progressive change: change which expands individual life chances, redresses historic inequities in well-being, and minimizes the subordination of some individuals and groups by others.

Strengths

The essay begins very strong. The story with which the applicant opens the essay is the most interesting part. This is fortunate because it immediately grabs the attention of the reader. Many work experiences are revealed throughout the essay that seem to have prepared the applicant well for law school.

Weaknesses

The essay would have been stronger if the applicant had remained in story-telling mode and let his experiences reveal his qualifications. The structure of the essay could have been improved if the applicant had created an outline. He refers to his resume in the essay, which is not advisable.

ESSAY 29: Naval Officer; Hispanic

Like many in my generation, I possess a strong desire to positively impact society in some way. However, my experience as a student in Mexico and later as a naval officer gives me a unique perspective and insight into the mentality of the average American that most students, scholars, and intellectuals do not have. Living in Mexico as a Hispanic, I was able to genuinely become part of Mexican society. This enabled me to view America from an outsider's standpoint. For the first time I objectively saw everything strong and beautiful and weak and ugly about American society and realized what aspects of it I wanted to help improve. Motivated, focused, and believing anything was possible, I was still plagued by naivete. This was quickly remedied by the traumas I experienced as a young naval officer.

Serving aboard a very small ship, I lead over twenty men for two years and advised and counseled them on every matter from the handling of debt to child care. I had to make their jobs worth coming to every day. It was a slow and very painful process learning that they work to live and not live to work. This realization did however provide me with the understanding of basic American values necessary to interpret laws written for the basic American. Designing policies and managing these men to complete complex tasks within the very restrictive framework of a large bureaucracy tempered my desires to improve society with the realization of what was possible.

Insight into basic American values was particularly important as neither of my parents have traditional American backgrounds. My father immigrated to America for religious reasons and my mother, though born in America in a rural Hispanic town, did not learn English until she was fifteen. Though not wholly meager, my background was not the fast track to a potential opportunity to attend a high caliber law school. I was the beneficiary of an excellent Utah public school system, the NROTC scholarship program (I lacked the financial resources to attend [school] without it), and the affirmative action program at [school] under which I believe I was admitted.

Though my above comments and statements and are what guide and affect me, I want to study law because I find it excruciatingly fascinating and overwhelmingly powerful. I feel my background, experience, and sincerity would make a fine contribution to the student body at [law school].

Strengths

The essay has interesting parts, particularly the more personal excerpts that describe the applicant's background.

Weaknesses

The essay is underdeveloped and has too many statements that are not backed up by examples. For instance, he claims in his opening sentence to want to impact society but never says how. Likewise, he does not demonstrate by example that he has given back to society thus far at any point in his life. This is actually something that admissions committees have specifically cited as a pet peeve in application essays—a bold statement of wanting to "help" with no evidence to support it. He also should have provided a more substantial reason for wanting to attend law school.

ESSAY 30: Issue Analyst; Gay Rights Activist

In December of 1988, Texas State District Court Judge Jack Hampton sentenced a man convicted of double homicide to a term of thirty years. After the hearing, Judge Hampton explained the light sentence with the statement "I don't care much for queers cruising the streets picking up teenage boys. I put prostitutes and gays at about the same level. If these boys had picked up two prostitutes and taken them to the woods and killed them, I'd consider that a similar case. And I'd be hard put to give somebody life for killing a prostitute."

Ideally, the American judicial system provides equal treatment to all parties. After working in the New York City jail system and the Manhattan District Attorney's Office, however, I am dismayed by the disparity between ideology and reality. The court system which should treat all individuals equally consistently falls short of this goal.

Because of various biases which exist within the court system, and within society as a whole, gays and lesbians in this country have historically been neglected or even persecuted by the law. In many ways, this neglect can be attributed to the social construct of the "closet." Because homosexuals in this country have been forced by society and the courts to suppress their own identities, their places within society are undermined. When gays and lesbians are told by society that they have a "lifestyle" rather than lives, and that this "chosen" lifestyle is abnormal and unacceptable, then they have been effectively forced out of society. Since the court system fails to address issues of discrimination in employment and housing, and neglects to punish perpetrators of hate crimes, gays and lesbians lose the one recourse which is supposedly guaranteed to all individuals. Justice Warren Burger writes in the Bowers v. Hardwick, 1986 decision, "condemnation of those practices [homosexual sodomy] is firmly rooted in Judeo-Christian moral and ethical standards . . . To hold that the act of homosexual sodomy is somehow protected as a fundamental right would be to cast aside millennia of moral teaching." When the highest court in the country condones the use of sexual orientation as a means to marginalize individuals, and people must conceal their identity to avoid societal discrimination, then gays and lesbians have truly lost their identities.

Although the judicial system has made progress in correcting its ills, it is impossible to deny that inequality in the application of justice still exists. As an individual considering a career in the law, I have a responsibility to recognize the disparity between ideology and reality, and to condemn it. Through obtaining a law degree, I hope to join many others in the struggle for our rights and dignity, and strive within an imperfect court system toward the goal of greater equality within the law.

Strengths

The essay has a strong and provocative beginning. It clearly sets the stage for an issue-themed essay and the opening quote will most likely cause individuals on either side of the issue to sit up and take notice. It is a well-written essay that demonstrates the conviction and political activism of the applicant. The applicant is perceived as someone who is truly motivated to obtain a degree in law.

Weaknesses

A potential weakness to some (but not to all) could be the lack of material about the applicant's background or future plans. Much of the essay is devoted to an issue, and not to the applicant's experiences, achievements, or goals. However, much can be concluded about the applicant from her discussion, so as long as the rest of her application is strong, this may not have been considered a weakness.

ESSAY 31: Family Background; Vietnamese; Public Service; Political Activist

When I was five years old, my family fled our homeland, the war-torn country of Vietnam. Though we left behind most of our personal possessions, we carried with us the cultural values that would profoundly influence our life choices. After arriving in the United States, my parents worked hard and prospered. We moved from a garage to an apartment to a condominium to a house within a six-year period on the wings of their industry and ambition. Yet my brothers and I never grew complacent, mindful that many of our friends and family continued to struggle. We saw our parents send money, hidden in the seams of clothing so that communist postal workers would not find it, to our relatives who remained in Vietnam; my father take two months' leave from his medical practice to rescue boat people in the South China Sea; and my mother establish a non-profit organization to assist newly arrived refugees.

These were not demonstrations of generosity as much as acts of duty. In Vietnamese culture, self-sacrifice is a virtue and one's obligation to others is paramount. Through their words and their deeds, our parents encouraged us to look beyond our own narrow interests and seek ways of helping others. As a result, they fostered in us a strong sense of social responsibility. I internalized this cultural conviction, adopting social good as a personal objective and exercising my talents in the service of others.

I have followed my parents' example by seeking opportunities both to develop my professional potential and to promote the social good. After graduating Phi Beta Kappa from the [school] I returned home and accepted a position with the district office of a state legislator that allowed me to cultivate valuable job skills and, at the same time, make a positive impact on my community. As a field representative for California Assemblyman T., I helped organize a successful health services fair for low-income Southeast Asians. This event brought county public health officials into Little Saigon to perform cholesterol and blood pressure screenings for adults and immunizations for children. In addition, I mobilized homeless activists throughout Orange County to pressure the Governor to reopen National Guard armories for use as emergency shelters during periods of cold weather. By working with local activists to expand the scope of social services at the local level, I fulfilled a personal and cultural imperative to serve the needs of others. Participating in these projects also enhanced my leadership, communication, and interpersonal skills.

Recently, I have applied these skills in a public service context through my involvement with federal legislative advocacy campaigns and my work for the American Bar Association's Section of Individual Rights and Responsibilities. When Congress took up consideration of immigration reform legislation last summer, I led a team assembled by the Women's Commission for Refugee Women and Children to lobby in favor of due process guarantees for asylum applicants and the deletion of a statutory cap on refugee admissions to the United States.

Since then, I have monitored congressional action on these and other issues for the ABA. In addition, as a Scoville fellow with the Union of Concerned Scientists, I worked with a coalition of peace and arms control organizations to preserve the international affairs budget from proposed cuts. These experiences have afforded me the opportunity to accomplish my aim of serving others. Furthermore, they have improved my research, writing, and advocacy skills. I have found, through my participation in these projects, that the focused efforts of dedicated volunteers and skilled professionals can produce just laws and wise policies. This recognition has, in turn, motivated me to apply to law school.

I look forward to utilizing the tools I will acquire in law school to advance the public interest more effectively. A law degree will enable me to play a more proactive role in shaping public policy by giving me the necessary skills to initiate changes to the legal code and to challenge unjust statutes directly. The specialized knowledge I will gain through a legal education will make me a better advocate for social good. Law school lies at the intersection of the work I have performed to date and the kind of work I wish to undertake. Obtaining a juris doctor will allow me to realize my intellectual potential, achieve my professional aspirations, and to continue to render meaningful service to others, thereby heeding my family values.

Strengths

The candidate has a lot of experiences that bode well for him in his application to law school and he has unveiled them successfully in this essay. While he packs a lot in, he never lists and he never sounds arrogant. He comes across as a humble individual who has a lot of experience that has both prepared him for law school and allowed him to help society. The essay is a good example of a candidate not simply claiming to want to contribute to society but demonstrating through his values, his upbringing, and his experiences that it is an honest endeavor. The essay has all the components of a successful application essay: solid writing skills, relevant experience that cannot be found elsewhere in the application, and a discussion of his motivation to study law and how the degree will enhance his career.

Weaknesses

None

ESSAY 32: Career Switcher; M.B.A.; Project Analyst

Since obtaining my M.B.A., the projects I've found most challenging and satisfying are those that would normally delegated to legal counsel. At my firm ("E."), however, our approach to deregulating and privatizing tightly regulated, capital intensive industries required that I, not counsel, analyze sophisticated contracts for loopholes and ambiguities, research and brief precedent setting legal questions, and decipher the complex laws that protect our environment and regulate defense procurement. These experiences, which are described below, have convinced me to pursue the credentials I'll need to do such rewarding work properly and over the long term.

The North Carolina Project:
I initiated this project by developing the nation's first non-utility peak power plant, and then offering to sell "Duke" $2.2 billion worth of power. After negotiating for six months, however, Duke's monopolistic tactics led E. to request assistance from the state utilities commission. This is when it became clear that my unique understanding of the state's utility regulations, and how they impacted the negotiations with Duke, required that I both testify before the commission and write the complaint and other filings in the case. Separately, this regulatory knowledge enabled me to craft the nation's first non-utility power plan license application based on the future power needs of the public, rather than on an executed contract with an existing utility.

My approach was to offer a lower cost to the public than Duke did, and then induce the presumably unbiased utilities commission, rather than Duke's management, to decide who would build the state's next major power plans. During the trial, the chairman of the commission was so impressed by my testimony, he commended me while on the record.

Duke countered by lowering its price to match E.'s, and this led the commission to deny our complaint and dismiss our license application, even though it had to adopt a new rule and apply it retroactively in order to do so. E. appealed both cases to the N.C. Court of Appeals, and I researched and wrote both briefs. Recently, when this court ruled against us by holding a key statute to be directory and not mandatory, I filed a petition for discretionary review with the Supreme Court of North Carolina. Although the ultimately outcome of the case remains unknown, I have thoroughly enjoyed this "once in a lifetime" experience and learned a lot about the law.

The M. Air Force Base (Florida) Project:

I began working on the development of the Air Force's first on-base energy privatization project. This novel contract provided for M. AFB to lease E. two plots of land on which to build, own and operate two privately financed cogeneration facilities. E. was then to supply $400 million of electric and thermal energy to the Air Force over a 30-year period.

In 1991 and 1992, I helped to modify the Air Force contract to make it financeable, and then negotiated the terms of the financing with the bank's attorney's at S.A. to protect my company's interests. In doing so, I used the skills I learned when analyzing the $276 million leveraged lease of an insolvent Texas power plant that I tried to acquire and restructure.

Shortly after the M. loan closing, and despite written Air Force representations to the contrary, E. learned that an ongoing Air Force activity on one of its leased sites was discharging hazardous waste into Tampa Bay. My ensuing investigation revealed that these discharges had been declared illegal by local regulators, that they had led the EPA to order contamination tests on the site (tests which the Air Force never performed), was prohibited without written EPA approval.

Upon learning this information, E. immediately halted site work and requested that the Air Force obtain the clearance required from the regulators so that construction could resume. The Air Force, however, inexplicably denied that any site testing was required and attempted to blame E. for any contamination ultimately found. This led E. to assert breach of contract and to lobby its representatives in Washington for help. A year later, with the assistance of Senators C. and A., the EPA gave its approval and construction resumed. During the stoppage, however, the Air Force breached E.'s contract in several other cases. I used this information to prepare a 340-page, $178 million certified claim that was later filed.

The preparation of the claim took about six months, and was particularly enjoyable because I got to use the skills I'd learned in North Carolina to explore the legal implications of the privatization relationship, determine how a maze of environmental regulations applied to E. and the Air Force on a federal enclave, and confirm that this case met the narrow criteria for anticipated profit recovery. Writing the claim was also exciting because I had internal Air Force documents that proved the contractual breaches, and because the very same group of personnel at the Air Force had just been severely reprimanded by an Armed Services Board of Contract Appeals ("ABSCA") judge for starting construction on the M. AFB golf course before obtaining the required environmental approvals, blaming the problem on the contractor, and then terminating his contract for default. This same judge was initially assigned to our case, but soon retired.

Given the magnitude and complexity of the claim, as well as the Air Force's self-incriminating documentation, the Air Force has yet to give any response to the claim other than a "general denial." Just as in the golf course case, however, it terminated our contract for default, asserting that construction should have proceeded without EPA approval. In November 1993, I wrote and filed a motion for summary judgement on the $178 million claim, as well as a complaint appealing the default termination. The Air Force has yet to respond to either filing.

Based on all of these matters, as well as on my recent role in acquiring a business through a bankruptcy court bidding war, I am confident that a career in law is something that I will both excel at and enjoy. I look forward to providing my clients with the focus and enthusiasm that my experience as a principal has taught me, qualities which I believe every attorney should have.

Strengths

The beginning clearly states how a legal degree will enhance the applicant's career. The projects that he describes as the essay progresses are further evidence that a legal degree would be a good fit for him and that he would likely succeed in law school. Since the applicant's work experience is probably the strongest aspect of his application, describing some of his projects was a smart tactic.

Weaknesses

The essay has a few grammatical errors and/or typos. The applicant is obviously a smart individual so the sloppiness indicates either a lack of time or a lack of attention to detail. The essay is also too long. Since the projects described are not examples of riveting storytelling, keeping their descriptions brief and thus cutting down the overall length of the essay would have been an improvement.

ESSAY 33: Social Activist; International Experience; Democratic Campaign Work

When I began my freshman year at [school], I did not expect that five years later I would find myself documenting a massacre in a guerrilla-controlled area of El Salvador and establishing a school there for refugees who had recently returned to their country. I also could not have imagined myself living in a community with no running water or electricity and hunting scorpions nightly before going to sleep. But that is where my interest in social action led me.

I went to Central America to see for myself the effects of the area's civil wars. First, I spent a month in Guatemalan refugee camps aiding Mama M., a refugee women's group. The refugees' continued commitment to improving their lives, despite 12 years of hardships, was an inspiration to me. I was similarly moved by the commitment of the people of El Sitio, a small rural community of repatriated refugees located in a guerrilla-controlled area of El Salvador. There a friend and I initially helped women from the community start a store in a tiny tin hut. The profits from the store went toward creating a day-care facility, providing the women with a place to leave their children while they built houses to replace those destroyed during the war.

My friend and I then established a much needed school in the community. I will always remember teaching our first class and handing out bags with paper, pencils, and scissors to 45 kids who were screaming with joy. For three months we lived in the community and taught reading, writing, and basic math, four times a day to both children and adults. After losing our final battle with unyielding immigration officials, however, we were forced to leave El Salvador. Before we left, we worked with nuns from the nearest town to ensure the school would continue with Salvadoran teachers.

Many of the Salvadoran war's victims were innocent civilians. I went, with a survivor, to the site where 120 relatives of the people of El Sitio had been massacred. Most of those massacred were either women or children. This powerful experience graphically demonstrated to me what can happen without a just political system. I interviewed community members, including some who had narrowly escaped the massacre, and gave their testimony to a lawyer working with the U.N. Truth Commission.

Even before Central America, I was involved in social action. At [school] I worked with the Massachusetts Public Interest Research Group (MASSPIRG) on the Toxics Use Reduction Act (TUR), an innovative plan to protect the environment and save businesses money by helping them reduce their use of toxic chemicals. I developed a political science independent study, which included working with MASSPIRG to finish the legislation and to create a strategy for lobbying Western Massachusetts state legislators to support the bill's passage. TUR was passed by the state legislature, and has since been used as a model by 12 other states. I was elected Chair of the [school] Chapter of MASSPIRG, and developed the chapter into the largest in MASSPIRG history and the most successful in the state.

Later, as President of the [school] student government, I worked to secure the establishment of mandatory prejudice reduction workshops for all freshmen and the adoption of a new [school] sexual harassment policy.

After my experiences in Central America, I worked in two elections for progressive Democratic candidates. I first joined Marjorie Margolies-Mezvinsky's campaign for the House of Representatives. We faced an uphill battle, as the Republican party had a 5 to 2 registration edge in the district and had represented it since 1916. Nevertheless, Margolies-Mezvinsky won the election.

Most recently I worked on the coordinated campaign in New Jersey to reelect governor Jim Florio and to elect Democrats to the state legislature. Along with a campaign manager, I was responsible for the policy, press, and fundraising for two state assembly races and one state senate race. I also served as the regional field director for Governor Florio's re-election campaign.

These experiences have broadened my understanding of social policy. I now want to go to law school to get the additional tools and analytical training I will need to help me in a career involving policy formation and implementation.

Strengths

The applicant tells very interesting and impressive stories from her past. They speak for her motivations, her compassion, her political activism, and her ability to lead and successfully complete challenging projects. It is a well-written essay that holds the attention of the reader, provides information that cannot be found elsewhere in the application, and creates an image of a person the reader might want to know. The essay provides supporting evidence (not just statements) that the applicant will succeed in law school.

Weaknesses

The final paragraph is underdeveloped. It is a weak conclusion to an otherwise strong essay. She could have improved the ending by expounding the discussion of her career plans.

ESSAY 34: Activist Since Childhood; Feminist/Woman's Activist; English Major

"That's not fair." Even as the smallest of children, I remember making such a proclamation: in kindergarten it was "not fair" when I had to share my birthday with another little girl and didn't get to sit on the "birthday chair." When General Mills changed my favorite childhood breakfast cereal, "Kix," I, of course, thought this was "not fair." Unlike many kids (like my brother) who would probably have shut up and enjoyed the "great new taste" or switched to Cheerios, this kid sat her bottom down in a chair (boosted by the phone book) and typed a letter to the company expressing her preference for the "classic" Kix over the "great new taste" Kix.

Through the plenty of "not fair" incidents that followed, my mother tried to explain that unfair things happen sometimes, but I never accepted the idea of an unfair world and began to realize that there were a great many situations and conditions that were "not fair" to women.

At age ten, I was mortified that all the boys in my Catechism class were signing up to be altar servers, but girls could not. When my grandmother told me that, at one time, because she was a woman, she was only allowed to touch the altar when she was *cleaning* it—the fight against the Catholic Church was on. Once again, I sat my bottom down in the chair (still with the phone book) and typed a letter to the Monsignor requesting to be trained as an altar server. With no immediate response, I respectfully but persistently harassed the Monsignor and the other priests every Sunday when I saw them in church, until, nearly two years later, I became an altar server. At age twelve I was almost too old to appreciate the new privilege, but there are girls becoming altar servers in that church to this day.

Fighting against things "not fair" for women has been my goal throughout my education, just as it will be in my future, and I have had several unique opportunities toward this end.

I have worked two summers in a Sacramento, California, law firm for the managing partner, a brilliant litigator and a woman who really cares about justice, on two of the biggest cases of her career. I performed legal research relevant to the issues of spoliation and antitrust, and I directly assisted Ms. F with trial preparation, accompanying her to court during the trials. Under her guidance I have learned the inner workings of litigation, and I have seen that unfairness pervades all types of law. Having experienced litigation, I know the heavy work load that characterizes trial preparation and can safely say that I approach a legal career aware of its realities.

I have also participated in the [school] Center for American Politics and Public Policy (CAPPP) Quarter in Washington program, which allowed me to take classes at the [school] Center and intern at the

National Women's Law Center in D.C. The Law Center showed me the public interest side of law, the area of law that I hope to enter in order to address the women's issues that are so important to me. Public interest offers the opportunity to help women who need it the most, those who could not otherwise afford legal assistance and who are often victims of the "not fair," of violations of their civil rights.

My classes at [school] and through CAPPP, as well as my participation in the volunteer program at the [school] Women's Resource Center, have afforded me the chance to research issues of the "not fair" for women. Violence against women, an unfairness that maims and rapes and kills, has evolved into a special interest of mine that I hope to pursue through future work in a sex crimes division in criminal prosecution. For two classes at [school] I have researched domestic violence and battered women who kill their abusers. While in Washington, D.C., I studied acquaintance rape among adolescents: after making an extensive review of the existing literature, I tried to conduct original research interviewing teenagers at a recreation center in Alexandria, Virginia.

Though at the last moment the recreation center directors did not authorize my project, I did discover a class called "Self-Defense is More than Karate" that was developed by the Office on Women in Alexandria to instruct high school students on relationships, HIV/AIDS, dating violence, and sexual assault. After I observed one week of the program, the Community Education Coordinator asked me to research how such education influences teens, interviewing students before and after they take the class, for the Office on Women. Currently, I seek a research grant from the [school] College Honors Program that would allow me to go back to D.C. in the spring to carry out this project.

Fighting the "not fair" is certainly a driving force for me; however, I have chosen to pursue law not only because I consider it to be a weapon against injustice, but also because it fascinates me. My love for the law echoes my love for literature. I participated in theater in high school and majored in English in college because I enjoy analyzing the subtleties, innuendos, and themes that serve as the foundation of a literary work or a dramatic performance. I strive to understand the stories behind the characters involved. I am awed by the power of language and the influence art and literature can have on the values, thoughts, and actions of the audience. So goes the influence on the law: they call it "courtroom drama" for a reason. Just as literature tells a story, so does each legal case, be it criminal or civil; the way in which the law applies to each case must be analyzed and, in some instances, constructed. Law reflects as much as it influences the beliefs of the people it governs.

Both law and literature are instruments of change. Furthermore, literature and law can give voice to people who have been traditionally silenced. Just as I love so much to hear the voices of others through literature, I want to use my voice in the realm of the law, calling out "not fair" for those who have not been heard. I want to have a positive influence on the lives of women and all people, be it in the civil or criminal realm, and in law school I hope to gain the tools to do just that.

Strengths

It is an interesting essay that reveals a lot about the personality of the applicant. She comes across as a strong individual who acts on her convictions and thus would do well as a lawyer. Her stories are entertaining and even though some took place before she was even 10 years old, she manages to make them relevant to the study of law. She weaves in later experiences that are further evidence of her preparation for and motivation to attend law school.

Weaknesses

The applicant overuses, and sometimes erroneously uses, quotation marks. Even though the term "not fair" was a prevailing theme of the essay, it too was overused and bordered on cutesy (not in a good way). Using it in the opening paragraph was effective but more grown up (and grammatically correct) language in the remaining essay would have been more appropriate.

While the essay was interesting for its entirety, the applicant should have respected the length requirements and kept it shorter. The essay has two themes: that much in life is "not fair" and that law and literature have much in common. Since the essay is too long, it may have been more effective to stick with only one theme because either could have carried the essay.

Essay 35: Religious Missionary in Argentina; Family Background

I realize the admission committee suggests a personal statement of no more than two double spaced pages, but in writing my statement, I found that in order to adequately convey even the smallest part of my two year mission experience I needed to write a little more. I hope the committee will sense the incredible significance of this time in my life and be understanding of my efforts to come to grips with it even though they have taken more than the requested length.

Just a few weeks after my freshman year at [school] ended I began my two year mission for the Church of Jesus Christ of Latter-Day Saints. It had been a difficult decision to leave the comfortable environment of [school] to go share my beliefs with people I did not know half a world away. There was a lot of pressure from my friends at [school] not to leave. A friend suggested, "If you really want to do this, why don't you wait until you graduate . . . You'll be more successful after having graduated from [school]." He did not understand. My mission was one of the only times in my life where I was able to escape the specter of institutionalized education. During my mission it did not matter that I attended [school], or even whether I had finished high school. What was important was my commitment to my beliefs. I had been looking forward to and saving for my mission for many years. Though I could not understand it at the time, I was embarking on a very different, but maybe even more important, kind of education.

I found myself in a tiny town called G., Argentina. While I was able to pick up quite a bit of Spanish during the two months I spent in the Missionary Training Center, my communications skills were still terribly lacking. I remember distinctly one night being incredibly frustrated because I could not adequately express myself. I remember thinking that words in any language were just not adequate to express the deep and poignant feelings I was experiencing. I eventually learned to communicate fluently in Spanish, but this frustration with the inadequacy of words to truly communicate feelings and experiences has remained with me to this day. More than ever I felt this frustration as I returned home from my mission and my friends and family asked me to tell them about my experiences. I soon found that regardless of how much I tried, words simply could not adequately express the depth or fullness of the intense personal, spiritual, social, and intellectual growth that my mission afforded me. Since I came home from Argentina more than two years ago, I have constantly struggled with the question of what the experiences of my mission mean to me and how to express their meaning. There are no easy answers, but I hope that through the exercise of this personal statement both you and I will be able to better understand the effect my mission has had on my life.

For two years I got up every day at 6:30 a.m. and spent all day, until I went to bed at 10:30 p.m. trying to help people. I lived in run-down buildings without heat and sometimes without running water. I did not go to any movies, watch TV, or even read the paper. At times it was difficult; I missed my home and my family. I missed my car and my girlfriend. My friends thought I was crazy when I left, and even since I have been home people still do not understand why I did what I did. But for me, my mission was one of the most important things I have ever done. It changed my life. The things I experienced and learned on my mission have effected me daily since that time and I believe that this will continue to be true for many years to come.

In many ways, my mission allowed me to get to know different aspects of myself and my culture. Though my father spoke Spanish before he learned English, Spanish was never spoken in my home. Even before my mission, I realized that by not being able to speak the language of my father's people I was missing part of myself. Every time we went to my grandparent's house or to the small Texas town of G. where my father was born and many of my relatives lived, I missed out on much of the discussion. My great-grandfather, who immigrated to the U.S. in 1909, farmed a small piece of land just outside G. and raised fighting roosters. I was sixteen before he died at the age of 97, but I never exchanged more than a smile and a head nod with this interesting old man. It was too late to change that particular case when I returned from my mission, but before my grandfather passed away last spring I was able to see that it made him proud to have a grandson who could speak Spanish. To this day, every time I see my grandmother (which is not often enough), she talks to me in Spanish, and I can tell that she is proud that I can understand our culture a little more. I am indebted to my missionary experience for allowing me to open up this part of myself.

The other ways that my mission effected me are more difficult to explain. Two years of daily dedication to missionary service changed my very being. Everything about me; my sense of right and wrong, my study habits, my relationship to my family and to others, even the way in which I viewed the world was altered in my two years in Argentina. H.V. was just one of the many people with whom I developed a special relationship during my time in Argentina. She was much poorer than anyone I have ever met in the United States, though I met many people in Argentina much poorer than her. But in addition to her being poor, there are also many other things I remember about her. In my journal I wrote, "I really love and respect her. I have never heard her complain . . . ", and "she is someone whose integrity I can always trust and in who I can always count on." Even though she was very hardworking, she lived in a little shack in what we would call a squatters camp along a polluted ditch, but she was proud of the few things she had. I also noted in my journal that she was always dressed neatly and her home was always very well kept. H.V. would save what money she could and invite us over for a meal of vegetable stew cooked over her hot plate. We would talk with her about the meaning of life while we ate our stew with stale bread as we sat on her mattress since she had only one little stool. Often the wind would whip through the holes in the walls and remind us of how cold it was outside. It was in those moments, and many more like them, that some part of me was changed. I was able to leave behind my world and my culture and somehow, if even for a few minutes, I was able to understand a perspective different from my own.

At some philosophical level, our society believes that everyone is equal, but at the same time, it constantly preaches the opposite—that some people are more important, that their opinions and experiences are more valid and valuable than others. Somehow experiencing life with people whose lives were very different than my own allowed me to actually feel that there are other ways to understand the world than the way I had been brought up. H.V. and many other people like her touched my life in ways that are impossible to explain, yet so profound that every part of my life has been changed by them. What I learned from her about different ways to view the world can extend even beyond the immediate details of that situation to include all different perspectives and experiences. The experiences of my mission constantly remind me that there are many different viewpoints and that the one which I have been accustomed to is not the only valid one.

Strengths

The essay has the potential to be interesting and it keeps the reader's attention by almost promising that something is going to happen. If nothing else, we get the sense that the applicant is a compassionate individual who is committed to justice for the underprivileged. We get this not from his words, but from his experiences.

Weaknesses

The essay never develops; it just keeps promising to. Even though his mission in Argentina is the topic of the essay, the applicant never explains what the goal of his mission was, how it changed him, or what it meant to him. In fact, he apologizes for the essay's length in the beginning because explaining all of the above would be difficult. The applicant should not have apologized for the length. Instead, he should have respected the length requirements. He should have been more effective at explaining all of what he set out to explain in the first place. Finally, he should have at least mentioned the words "law school" at some point.

ESSAY 36: Philosophy Major; Student Leader; Humor Writer; Software Consultant; Law Intern; Victim of Crohn's Disease

The guide for much of my life has been education, and my education has taken varied forms. I chose [college] not only because of the National Merit and Regents Scholarships it offered me, but also because of the scope of its curriculum. Unlike some other major research institutions, [college] demands breadth in the learning of each of its students.

A saying among us is, "At [college], we do it because it's required"—although, of course, these are requirements that we have willingly accepted. I think specifically of the interdisciplinary humanities sequence. In addition to being valuable in itself, it confirmed that a Philosophy major was the proper choice for me.

Philosophy offers freedom for intellectual exploration not available in many other academic disciplines—I have taken advantage of this opportunity through my Areas of Concentration. And to satisfy some of my other academic interests I have minored in Law & Society and History. The Law & Society minor, although not only for those planning on going to law school, has helped me to decide that I should pursue a career in law. In addition to it and my History minor, which has allowed an exploration of ideas similar to philosophy's but with its own particular perspective, I have taken a number of sociology and political science classes outside of my major and beyond [college] breadth requirements. I have found all these courses valuable because, even when not required of me, they expanded and deepened my outlook.

My participation in [college's] extracurricular activities has resulted in another sort of education. The most rewarding has been my time on the [college] Council. The Council acts as the supervisory committee for student groups that are part of the Dean's and Provost's offices. It has direct contact with students and with college staff and faculty. Because we, as students, planned and performed the projects ourselves, and were therefore responsible for the results, good or bad, being a part of the Council gave me the feeling of true accomplishment. This year, after a two-year appointment to the campus-wide Registration Fee Committee, I have returned to [college] leadership program and am a member of the Judicial Board and Graduation Committee; I hope once again to make an impact and feel the satisfaction that comes from working at my college. In addition to these leadership-related activities, I have been a writer for the *Koala*, the humor newspaper. The paper's content varies from standard comedy to satire, from the innocent to the off-color, and the staff represents a cross section of the campus not seen inside any one classroom. The *Koala* is the most-read and best-loved paper at [college], and being a part of its staff has not only made me aware of the effort that goes into publishing a newspaper, but has also shown me a facet of university life with its own value, different from that of academic and leadership activities.

While attending [college] and participating in its extracurricular opportunities, I have also worked part time as an independent contractor-consultant to Touch Technologies, Inc. (TTI). At this software development firm I have often acted as the assistant to the Vice President of Operations. When I started my employment at TTI, the Vice President said that, in addition to learning the technical aspects of the job, I would learn equally important lessons about the functioning of a small company.

My time at TTI has allowed me to discover much about the running of a business—including the important relationships that exist between management and workers and among workers themselves. I consider all these lessons to be valuable. As an outgrowth of my consulting at TTI, I have worked as an independent desktop publisher. The professional demands of being self-employed in this way have rewards of their own—it has required that I manage the expenses, incomes, operations, and productions that every small business owner must consider. Through TTI and this other work, I have been both employee and employer, and have learned the responsibilities and freedoms that come with each.

Among the future activities to which I look forward for educational and other benefits are the internships in which I will soon participate. This winter quarter I will be interning with the law firm of [name]. As a part of this interdisciplinary firm of business, personal injury, and criminal law, I will be trained in legal research and writing, client interviewing, and observing in a courtroom setting. I think it is very desirable that students considering a career in law first gain a practical understanding of law practice. This is the main reason that I have pursued this opportunity. Similarly, for the spring quarter I have applied for and been offered internships with the United States Senate Committee on the Judiciary and the [name] Company, a political consulting firm. To choose between them is a dilemma—each offers a view of our government from a different perspective—but it is a choice which I am pleased to face.

There is one more important part of my life that has provided me with another sort of education: my experience as a person with Crohn's disease. I was diagnosed with Crohn's, a gastrointestinal disease, in the sixth grade. Developing this chronic disease at such a young age has understandably had serious affects upon me, both physically and emotionally. Yet I can honestly say that having Crohn's has not been wholly negative. The restriction of certain freedoms has caused me to channel my energies into other creative outlets, including scholastic, professional, and personal ones. Because of it I have been forced to approach life differently than others my age, with reflections and conclusions informed by a unique perspective. As much as anything else, living with Crohn's disease has been a valuable form of education. I try to apply what I have learned from it to other aspects of my life and to the lives of others with whom I am in contact, knowing that there is always a solution to what at first may seem insoluble.

My activities in school and in the school leadership and extracurricular community, my work both as an employee and as someone self-employed, my law-related plans prior to entering law school, and personal considerations should highlight that my interests are truly diverse.

Strengths

The essay presents a thorough account of what the applicant has done from the time he entered college until the moment of applying to law school.

Weaknesses

The strength stated above could also be viewed as a weakness. The applicant recounts far too much information about college work and extracurricular activities that can be found elsewhere on the application. The first two paragraphs could be left out of the essay altogether, as they provide nothing substantial. The experiences mentioned that would apply directly to law school, are activities that have not even commenced yet; therefore, too much time is devoted to them in the essay. The mention of having Crohn's disease is not integrated meaningfully into the essay. The ending is very weak and almost offensive to the reader—highlighting what the reader *should* infer from what the applicant has revealed about himself is not an effective tactic. This applicant most likely had a very high GPA and LSAT score because, while this essay obviously did not hurt him, it is doubtful that it would have enhanced his application.

ESSAY 37: Public Affairs Intern; Crohn's Disease

By the spring of 1994, I had completed my coursework required to graduate from [school], and consequently had the quarter free to do with as I wished. With this extra time available, I decided to go to Washington, D.C., and intern on Capitol Hill. Traveling to the capital was an exciting prospect for me because I have always loved American political history and wanted to explore the city where so much of it has occurred.

In school, I had enjoyed and gotten satisfaction from minoring in Law and Society and from clerking in a law office. I figured that going to Washington, the city where our laws are made, would help me confirm my decision to become an attorney, and I was not disappointed.

Choosing The Keefe Company (TKC) was not easy, as I was also offered a position with the Senate Judiciary Committee. Although that committee would have been particularly interesting to me as an intended lawyer and as one who has long taken an avocational interest in law, I was told that I would have to spend much of my time doing clerical chores. On the other hand, TKC, a government relations and public affairs firm, offered almost entirely substantive activities. So, although I regretted not having the "glamour" of working on the Hill on an important committee, I did not regret the choice that I made. During the spring, my major project was producing a monthly report on U.S. political and economic policy toward Asia for an Asian client; this was a new contract for TKC, and I found it exciting to be involved in the major research and activity that accompanied its beginning. I kept abreast of daily developments in Asia, read government and non-government organization (NGO) documents, attended Congressional hearings, and contacted government and NGO officials who are experts on the U.S.'s Asian policy. I also researched telecommunications issues, primarily those pertaining to the FCC auctions of spectrum for personal communications services. That project was especially interesting because it involved one-on-one contact with TKC clients. Through both projects I gained insight into how Washington really works, from the initial desires of individuals, groups, and companies, to how those wants and needs are finally played out in legislation and policy.

I especially do not regret choosing TKC now, because I currently live in Washington, having been hired by the company following my internship; the chairman offered me a job shortly after I informed him of my intention to take a year off before going to law school. I made that decision because I felt that working in the "real" world for a while would be as valuable as my formal education and make me a better law school student. My responsibilities at TKC have increased even more in the past few weeks, because we have begun a fundamental restructuring: the company's focus has shifted to international business and direct consulting with foreign governments and government officials; one of the partners left to become Ambassador to Chile; and the Executive Leadership Council, a national organization of African-American business leaders founded by our President, moved to new headquarters. I am now a supervisor of the interns, and am also working much more closely with the Chairman and the company's clients, including International Public Relations, a Japanese consulting firm, and the governments of the Dominican Republic and Paraguay. The change has been somewhat unsettling, but I have welcomed the greater duties and involvement that it has brought.

Being part of The Keefe Company is important to me not just because of the experience I am gaining, but because this is the first time I have lived away from home for an extended period of time. In spite of offers from more prestigious universities, I went to [school] largely because I have Crohn's disease. Crohn's is a gastrointestinal disorder, and I was diagnosed with it in the sixth grade. Without going into the details about how it affects me on a daily basis, I can say that mentally it has caused me to become more introspective, while physically it has affected what I do, where I go, and whom I meet. It was because of Crohn's that I had

---

NOTE: Essays 36 and 37 were written by the same applicant. Essay 36 was submitted prior to accepting the Keefe internship.

not been to Washington earlier, as I was hospitalized just a few days before my eighth grade class trip here. That was one of my many stays in the hospital, which were also accompanied by numerous operations. Luckily, I have recently been in something of a remission from Crohn's, one that gave me the courage to leave the comforts of home and to come here to Washington.

However, while the disease is currently not very active, I continue to suffer from its lingering effects and must say that Crohn's is the defining element of my life. Developing this chronic ailment at such a young age understandably had, and continues to have, serious effects upon me. Yet by no means would I say that having Crohn's disease has been wholly negative. As is common with people who have something terrible happen to them, I feel that Crohn's has made me a better, or at least a different, person. The restriction of certain freedoms has caused me to channel my energies into other outlets, including creative and personal ones. I am sure that my reflective nature—friends frequently tell me that I "think too much"—is at least partly an outgrowth of my disease, and also that it contributed to my study of philosophy in school. Because of Crohn's, I have been forced to approach life differently than my peers, and I believe it has given me insight, drive, and a distinct focus—I have always tried to find solutions to problems that at first seemed unsolvable. As much as anything else in my life, having Crohn's disease has been a valuable education, and I have tried to apply what I have learned from it to other aspects of my life.

It is such thoughts, along with my formal education and my professional experiences here in Washington, that I believe would make me a valuable addition to [name of law school]. I hope that you feel the same.

NOTE: This essay was written by the same applicant who wrote essay 36 after completing an internship that was mentioned in the previous essay.

Strengths

Wow—what a difference! This essay is far superior to the essay that the applicant wrote prior to the internship that is the theme of the essay. It is not because of the internship experience; it is because in this essay the topic is about something that cannot be found directly on the application. It is true that he has a topic to write about that is more relevant to law school but the point is more that he finally reached outside of his college experience to offer something new of himself to the admissions committee. The writing is better and more succinct, which is another improvement. The applicant's discussion of having Crohn's disease is better integrated into this essay. His reflections on how the disease has impacted his life offers something personal about him, something that the previous essay lacked.

Weaknesses

The topics covered could have been discussed in fewer words, leaving more room to explain why the applicant wants to go to law school and what his plans are for the future.

ESSAY 38: Overcoming Childhood Obstacle; Explaining Poor Early Record

If a reporter were to write an article on my collegiate career, it would tell an impressive story. It would include a list of co-curricular activities only matched by my involvement in community politics. My academic achievements at [school] would be summed up in my Dean's List placement. The reporter would probably break up the serious academic bend by touching on how I founded and published [school's] first humor magazine, the film I directed, or the fact that I was a guitarist and songwriter for a hard rock band. The article would present a well-rounded individual, and the reader would probably walk away with the idea that I have always been self-determined, ambitious, and self-confident. This may be the case now, but it is certainly not the whole story.

I was a short, thin fifth grader with a humiliating bionator jutting from my mouth. I would often be greeted by my "friends" after school, their shirts pulled over their legs, on their knees, weebling and wobbling around, calling me worthless, and singing Randy Newman's infamous song, "Short People Have No Business . . ." Reflecting on situations like that now bring a wry smile to my face, but in actuality, that constant stream of acidic ridicule at such an early age took a heavy toll on me. I was confused. I had been taught by my parents invaluable tools such as self-respect through achievement and scholarship, and pride and integrity through accomplishing goals. But even though I used these tools in my junior high years (honor roll both years, class president, lead actor in two school plays), I still was being harassed, constantly being bombarded with put-downs. It became overwhelming to the point where my parents' teachings could no longer help me deal with my lack of self-confidence.

Upon entering high school, I created a subconscious plan: make everyone like me so that they would ignore my literal shortcomings. I had always been extremely creative, I had always been considered to have a good sense of humor, so why not use these talents to compensate for that detachment and marginality that I felt deep down? I transformed myself from Junior High Achiever to High School Demagogue in one year.

My public attempts to seek forgiveness for my inadequacies became my priority, and the school work and scholarship, once a source of great distinction, became secondary. I was still a drooling wreck inside, a depressed fool, but on the outside I was a carefree joker. I got the popularity I wanted, I was even overwhelmingly voted Senior of the Year, but my popularity was devoid of any dignity, any sense of respect.

Upon graduating my grades were so poor, my dreams of a college career seemed impossible. I completely hated the person I had become, playing to the crowds and prostituting my talents for cheap praise. I realized that I had let myself down, I had failed to fulfill my potential, and had used my talents to defeat myself. In those miserable days I swore that I would change my life around. I found this source of rejuvenation in what I knew all along, self respect through achievement and scholarship, and integrity in achieving goals.

During my early years at [school], I had to re-teach myself how to study, to learn, to achieve again. That semester was an incredible rebirth for me. My smile was no longer fake, the happiness I felt was real. My first semester grades were only a 2.7, but it was a step in the right direction. I dedicated myself to physical fitness, and started to become proud of my physical appearance, which helped to improve my mental state as well.

Today, I am at [school], a school that I used to dream of attending. I not only believe that I have excelled at this level, but feel that I am where I should have been all along, at the top academically, living up to my potential and pushing myself with new challenges. Now it is time for me to tackle another challenge, and that is to study law. In recent years, I have been attracted to the ambiguity of law, the creativity that is involved in its execution, and its ever-changing face. I believe there are few other professions that can reconcile both my scholarly and creative drive that for the last few years have propelled me to success.

If I were to write an article on myself, it would be one of overcoming self-inflicted personal adversity, becoming the person I always knew I could be, and ending with a successful first year of law school.

Strengths

This is a great essay. It is entertaining and personal. It shows that the applicant is both confident and humble and that he can overcome adversity. It demonstrates that he can succeed when he wants to—and the fact that he now wants to is clear. It doesn't have much to do with law school but that is not problematic. He is explaining who he is, which is what the committee wants, and he does manage to integrate why the study of law is important to him.

Weaknesses

Using a reporter's hypothetical words to describe himself was a bit gimmicky. He may have chosen a cleverer manner to reveal himself, but while it wasn't perfect, it was still pretty good.

ESSAY 39: Cancer Survivor; Volunteer; Applicant for Joint JD./ M.B.A. Program; Management Experience; International Experience

I have always been a self-motivated person, someone who enjoyed working hard to produce results. I also took life for granted, assuming that the next day would always arrive on time. However, the relative importance of life itself to the events that compose it did not become clear to me until my sophomore year of high school. That was the year that I was diagnosed with an unusual type of lymphoma, cancer of the lymph system. CANCER. The word that everyone shied away from became a living reality for me in the middle of my high school career. Now, more than six years after the diagnosis—fulfilling the technical definition of being "cured"—and with the world of chemotherapy far behind me, I still view conquering this disease as the largest achievement of my life.

My battle with a serious illness led me to reflect on the positive aspects of the fight. In particular, I realized that it was important for me to share my experience with others who were in similar situations. This feeling led me to work as a pediatric hematology peer consultant at [school] medical center. My goal was to counsel and talk with children and young adults who had cancers and other serious illnesses. The work was particularly rewarding because it provided people with a new resource, giving them insight and comfort during a difficult period.

The sense of strength and independence that came from my battle with cancer carried over into my summer employment of two years at the Ann Arbor Center for Financial Services, a small company composed of attorneys, trust and estate planners, and financial analysts. During my time there, I compiled complete financial reports and portfolio analyses for our wealthy clients (whose individual net worths exceeded $1 million), leading to extensive changes in asset allocation that greatly improved the overall return on their holdings. Additionally, my management skills were particularly tested for a two-week period, during which time I ran the office alone due to vacations and illnesses of the other company professionals. I was also exposed to many legal situations in this position, ranging from compliance with SEC regulations to drafting living wills and durable powers of attorney. It was a valuable combination of business and law, and inspired me to apply to the joint JD/MBA program.

A second job that combined the challenges of business and law was the business manager position of WPRB (a 30,000 watt commercial radio station—103.3 FM). From the business viewpoint, as manager of forty-seven advertising accounts, organization was a key factor for success. I saw the station increase profits by over 100 percent, while simultaneously spending over 300 percent more on capital improvements. I also diversified our available funds into three separate interest-bearing accounts, in an attempt to spread risk and improve our overall returns. As part of a power upgrade later in the year, I redesigned our accounting system to incorporate all of the changes in our assets. Lastly, a switch to mail order suppliers dramatically increased the cost efficiency of our offices.

The position at WPRB also involved many legal issues. For example, I negotiated settlements on the two largest, inherited, overdue accounts, narrowly avoiding costly court battles. Also, the contracts for our sales accounts needed to be redesigned to include the changes necessitated by our power upgrade. Finally, I ensured that FCC regulations were constantly followed and that changes in these rules were monitored and incorporated into our station's format.

A third challenge to both business and law skills was presented through the founding of my own musical entertainment company, [name]. This independent venture began in the fall of 1988, with two employees and no capital. Today, I have four employees, am affiliated with the largest entertainment agency on the East coast (East Coast Entertainment), have three regional 800 numbers, and work all types of events from Washington D.C. to New York. The company's fixed assets now exceed $20,000. I designed the legal contract for this company, cleared it with three local legal advisors, and currently handle all marketing and promotions with the aid of the other employees. The time commitment to the company is large (twenty hours/week or more), but the rewarding experience of running my own company makes every minute worthwhile.

I have always had a strong interest in other cultures—in particular, how different cultural upbringings lead to different situational responses. Because my mother is Swiss, I have been fortunate to have immediate family whose experiences and reactions to events are entirely different from my own. Speaking with my uncle or grandparents about the European perception of American policies and politics always fascinates me. My studies have included six years of German language instruction, not only to prepare for the possibility of practicing international law or business, but also to communicate with my family in their own language. A second opportunity to experience other cultures occurred, when I entered the Yeats international summer school in Sligo, Ireland. This poetry workshop included students from all over Europe, Asia, and the United States. Through this program, I learned more than just Irish writing and poetry—I was exposed to a whole world of ideas and perspectives on everything from habits to world events to different ways of thinking.

I realize that I am strongly motivated by a desire to succeed personally, to better the current system, to help those with illnesses and other misfortunes, and to find innovative ways of achieving my goals. This work ethic has a tendency to be contagious, often inspiring others to do the same. A graduate degree in law and business would enable me to continue to pursue these goals.

Strengths

The essay begins strong. The applicant's fight and victory over cancer is personal and inspiring. It demonstrates determination and an ability to overcome obstacles. She successfully unveils her work experiences (otherwise not directly related) as relevant to her preparation to attend law school.

Weaknesses

Her transition to the paragraph that introduces a new topic, her interest in other cultures, is awkward. She does not successfully tie it in to the rest of the essay, let alone the paragraph that precedes it. Her ending is weak and comes across as a forced and rapid conclusion.

ESSAY 40: Naval Service; Family Background (Romanian); Father's Influence; Religious Christian

The black nuclear powered submarine smoothly glides beneath the waves. Seated in the diving officer's chair in the dark control room, I scan the ship's control panel, carefully monitoring the depth gauges and the ship's angle indicator. With the ship properly on course, my thoughts turn to the bearing of my own life.

My latest assignment had rushed upon me. Taken out of submarine school a week early and hastily flown first to Hawaii and then Japan, I suddenly found myself aboard my new submarine. Facing the commencement of a demanding six-month deployment to be followed by a Supply Management Inspection (SMI), the crucial periodic evaluation of the supply department, I remained resolutely optimistic. Several of my instructors at the Navy Supply Corps School had confided that my exceptional academic performance had placed me in this billet aboard a submarine that had failed the previous inspection. They called this "an opportunity to excel." Although newly married and not excited at the prolonged separation, I regarded the extended tour as an opportunity to reshape the unorganized supply department into a winning team.

As Supply Officer, I was both a junior officer and a department head directly responsible to the captain for all supply matters. A young ensign, fresh from Naval ROTC, the only way to convince the captain that I could handle the responsibility of feeding the crew of 150 and managing an inventory of over 20,000 line items, all while standing daily watches and working toward my submarine qualifications, was by doing it. I worked assiduously at sea and in port, spending long weeks in Guam working past midnight and through the weekends while my fellow junior officers enjoyed learning how to scuba dive. My efforts proved fruitful. Not only did the ship pass the SMI, but it received better than average grades! In turning an unsatisfactory operation into an above average one, I had finally gained the captain's complete confidence and was rewarded with a Navy Achievement Medal. The Navy's announcement that experienced lieutenants, instead of young ensigns, would be assigned to attack submarines in the future only heightened the significance of this achievement.

Although now readily accepted as the expert authority for all supply matters, I still found frequent opportunity to practice my negotiating and persuasive skills. As local advocate for all external supply dealings I had to account for the efficiency of the entire supply system. The experience of many successful high school debates combined with negotiation skills developed through [school] consulting and entrepreneurial management courses fed my self-assurance. My familiarity with supply publications developed to the point where I could quote obscure passages from memory. In response to my captain's query about the admissibility of procuring hotel rooms while visiting Brisbane, Australia, I was able not only to paraphrase all pertinent regulations, but also to suggest a good hotel.

"We are too light, Diving Officer," grumbled the helmsman, tumbling me out of my reverie. I glance at the ship's angle indicator and direct the Chief of the Watch to bring 4,000 pounds of sea water into the ballast tanks. The ship is still on course, but my career is nearing a turning point.

My obligated naval service is complete and I look forward to beginning law school. I must pursue a legal career both to serve my personal convictions and also to complete my father's unfulfilled dream. My father, [name], completed only two years of law school in Bucharest, Romania before his anti-communist activities and temporary imprisonment prevented him from completing his legal education. My Christian faith requires me to serve my community to the best of my ability. I hope to exercise my commitment to community service through occasional pro bono work for Christian legal organizations such as John Whitehead's Rutherford Institute.

Strengths

This essay starts off strong. Through his experiences as a naval officer on a submarine, the applicant demonstrates that he is intelligent, responsible, and capable both as an individual problem solver and as a manager. His ability to succeed in law school was likely not questioned.

Weaknesses

The essay takes an awkward turn toward the end. The second to the last paragraph is oddly out of place. It is not connected to the paragraphs that precede it or to the final paragraph that follows it. The idea of concluding the essay with a discussion of why the applicant is now applying to law school is logical but the reasons he gives do not formulate a strong conclusion. To state that one's motivation to attend law school is to fulfill a parent's dream (no matter the reason) is not advisable. Nor is it recommended to state that any desire to serve one's community stems from a "requirement" of his or her religion. These issues make the ending weak and the applicant's motivations questionable. The essay would have been stronger had the final two paragraphs been excluded.

ESSAY 41: Criminal Justice Major; Police Officer (2 years); Accepted at the University of Michigan

Simply stated, I am very proud of what I accomplished in my four years at XXX University. I am not proud because my résumé brings many compliments or because some of my achievements have brought me widespread recognition. Instead, I am proud that I first had the courage to set such lofty goals for myself and that I successfully reached those objectives by maintaining an unyielding motivation. While these goals were not always tangible in nature, the underlying principle was to take advantage of every opportunity afforded to me and to give a 100% effort to every endeavor that I undertook. Upon matriculating, my first obligation was obviously to my studies. My first semester began with a 4.0 report card and my dedication to sustaining that level of prosperity resulted in a final grade point average of 3.9. This is clearly a noble achievement in itself; however, I would not have been satisfied in simply sitting on my laurels.

My first extracurricular activity was working for the recreation department as an intramural sports official. Though the work was less than glorious, it immediately became an enjoyable hobby—which I happened to get paid for. My interest in officiating grew, along with my experience and abilities. I was soon selected to referee in the Flag Football National Championship Tournament in New Orleans. I quickly ascended the local ranks as a high school baseball, basketball, and football official. My expertise was ultimately rewarded with a promotion to Head Supervisor of Intramural Recreation.

During one of our recreation basketball tournaments, I was appointed to handle the public address system. I did nothing more than have fun. The following week, I found myself behind the microphone once again, this time as the Public Address Announcer for the XXX University Women's Basketball Team. After gaining some notoriety that season, my duties expanded over to the Men's Basketball Team and the Bulldog Hockey Squad, including games against the University of Michigan Wolverines—the NCAA National Champions, I should note. Further assignments included many on-campus events, the Great Lakes Intercollegiate Athletic Conference Basketball Championship, the Michigan High School Athletic Association Basketball Quarterfinals, and the Pepsi Hockey Holiday Tournament at the Grand Rapids Van Andel Arena, Home of the International Hockey League "Griffins."

At that time, I was studying to become a police officer, so I was elated when I was eventually hired as a police dispatcher. My affiliation with the Department of Public Safety also grew into a Service Officer position (a.k.a. "The Guy Who Writes All Those Damn Parking Tickets On Campus," a hero and mainstay at any college). Both jobs were intrinsically rewarding and provided many very valuable educational and professional experiences. As my number of occupations continued to grow, I did not cutback on my time at any job. So, obviously, my time was very much taken up by school and work.

Despite my good grades and my notable vocations, I felt that there was still something lacking. It was during a campus-wide recruitment for student organizations that I realized what was missing. I did not hesitate in joining the XXX State University Beta Kappa Rho Chapter of the American Criminal Justice Association—Lambda Alpha Epsilon (ACJA-LAE), though I was the only freshman to do so that year. As I became more familiar with the objectives of this professional fraternity, my dedication to its ideals also grew. As a freshman, I was pleased to have been nominated for the Executive Board, though I did not win the election. In my sophomore and junior years, I served as a committee chairperson and chapter Treasurer. During my four years of membership, I saw the fraternity grow to be one of the largest student organizations on campus and in my senior year, I was elected their President.

My extensive experiences were rewarded in my junior year, when I was nominated and accepted in my first year of eligibility into Omicron Delta Kappa—The National Leadership Honor Society. Again, I became immediately active and was chosen as a delegate to the national conference the following spring. Just as suddenly, I was unanimously elected as President of the Ferris Circle for my senior year. While I could also be found serving in numerous other student organizations or committees, I was always fully dedicated to applying my aptitudes to attaining the aims of the group.

I strongly feel that the many skills that I gained through student leadership and organizations provided me with some of the most valuable educational experiences in my time at Ferris. While reflecting on those accomplishments, I would often look around—in vain—for someone to pat me on the back with a hardy "Atta-Boy!" Nonetheless, I would learn from the inherent rewards of each feat and gather the motivation to meet my next set of goals. I was perfectly content in this system of achievement to the very eve of my graduation, when I was surprised with the "Eagle Award" at the Criminal Justice Senior Banquet. Before a packed ballroom at the Holiday Inn, the presenter outlined each of my accomplishments, including many that I thought had previously gone unnoticed. In just a few short minutes in that room, I quickly realized an entirely new dimension to my hard work and perseverance.

It was during my junior year that I first noticed my strong comprehension of criminal law and procedure. Since then, I knew that law school was a viable option for my future. While I have thoroughly enjoyed serving the last year as a police officer in XXX Township, it has become more and more apparent that I am searching for a greater challenge. So, it was with great conviction that I set forth to best prepare myself for the LSAT and, as a result, I ultimately exceeded my own expectations with a score of 170. Now, I feel that I am very ready to enter the academic environment, once again, and I look forward to continuing my strong scholastic ethic in law school. I truly cannot think of any better place for me to begin setting goals for my legal career than at The University of Michigan.

Strengths

The applicant demonstrates that he excels in most tasks that he attempts. His experiences and associations give the impression that he is prepared for and can succeed in law school.

Weaknesses

The essay is too long and is a bit dry. Some of the paragraphs read like lists of achievements or associations. The applicant doesn't seize the opportunity to break away from his college experiences and tell the admissions committee something about himself that cannot be found elsewhere on his application.

Essay Index

Index

How to
Succeed in
Law
School

Fourth Edition

Gary A. Munneke

Associate Dean,
Law Placement Division
of Pace University,
New York City

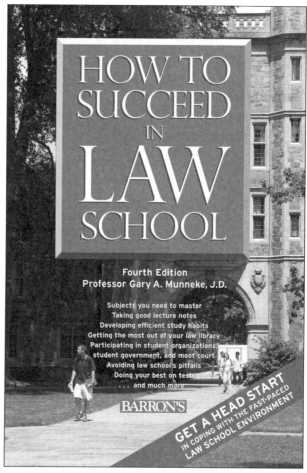

240 pages, paperback, ISBN: 978-0-7641-3979-6

This is the book that shows students how to use the highly competitive law-school environment to their very best advantage! Instead of feeling overwhelmed by all the pressure, they'll learn what steps to take for feeling in control. Expert techniques for researching, notetaking and studying, tips on using library resources, solid advice on coping with various kinds of stress, and even pointers on time management and personal finances are covered. Plus, readers will value the helpful index.

Please visit **www.barronseduc.com**
to view current prices and to order books

Barron's Educational Series, Inc.
250 Wireless Blvd.
Hauppauge, N.Y. 11788
Call toll-free: 1-800-645-3476

In Canada: 1-800-247-7160
Georgetown Book Warehouse
34 Armstrong Ave.
Georgetown, Ontario L7G 4R9

(#21) R1/08

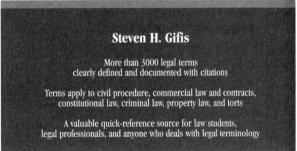

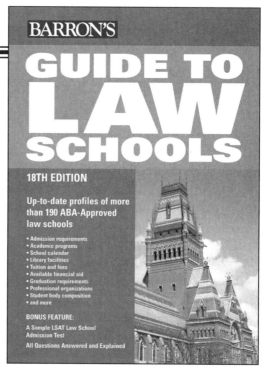